THE BOYS' BOOK OF WHALERS

IN A SPECIAL BUILDING WAS A MODEL OF A FAMOUS WHALER

THE BOYS' BOOK OF WHALERS

By
A. HYATT VERRILL
Author of " Radio for Amateurs," "An American Crusoe," " The Real Story of the Whaler," etc.

WITH ILLUSTRATIONS BY THE AUTHOR

WILDSIDE PRESS

ILLUSTRATIONS

	PAGE
In a special building was a model of a famous whaler	*Frontispiece*
When the whale is at last alongside the dirtiest and hardest work of all begins	30
Before long the last old Yankee whale ship will be but a memory of the past	30
Her dingy patched sails were bellying out like dun-colored balloons	52
These boats are the most seaworthy and safest small boats which were ever designed or built	52
Explanation—Kinds of whales, symbols, etc.	88
Explanation—Implements and weapons used in whaling	138
The reason for the decline of the whaling industry was the drop in prices of whalebone and whale oil	198
They had been through three winters in the arctic to secure the full cargo of oil	198

THE BOYS' BOOK OF WHALERS

CHAPTER I

"THAT'S the queerest looking craft I've ever seen," declared Harry Bennet as he turned from a long survey of the strange vessel on the horizon ahead.

The yacht, on which Harry was cruising, was tacking across the mouth of Buzzard's Bay and the ship which had attracted his attention was coming out of the Bay before the brisk northerly wind. Her dingy patched sails were bellying out like dun-colored balloons; a little mountain of white water was about her high, bluff bows and her lofty sides towered, like the walls of a house, far above the green waves. Her low, stout masts, immensely long and heavy spars, uptilted bowsprit and ornate figure-head gave her a very ancient appearance, and through his glasses,

Harry had noticed that her davits were crude wooden affairs, and that there were numerous boats swinging from them.

At Harry's words, the sailing-master,—an old salt from Cape Cod,—turned and squinted at the vessel. "Aye, I reckon ye ain't seed many o' sech craft," he remarked. " Yonder's a whaler,—reg'lar old timer too. New Bedford ship. I ain't seed none o' her kind fer nigh twenty year. Reckon the war's made ile go so sky-high they're a-fittin' out o' all the ol' hookers."

"A whaler!" exclaimed Harry. "Why, I thought whaling was a thing of the past,—that is, in these waters. Of course I knew the Scotch had steam whaling ships in the Arctic and that on our Pacific coast they killed whales with guns and towed them to refineries by tugboats. Say, Captain, run over near so we can have a good look at her. My, but she's a funny old tub!"

Shifting the helm a point or two, Captain Ned eased off the yacht's sheets and the little yawl tore through the water towards the bark.

Presently, they were within hailing distance and Harry noted with interest the details of the whaling ship. She was bark-rigged, but short and tubby and seemed to have a deck cluttered and littered with all sorts of odds and ends, while the crew, or at least those who stared curiously at the passing yacht, looked far more like a crowd of tramps and gutter snipes than like sailors.

By now, Harry's father, and his cousin Bob, had come from below and all three watched the old bark as she bobbed and plunged along on her course.

Captain Ned hailed her through a megaphone, asking her name and where bound, and a tall, lanky man, with ragged beard and a stiff Derby hat, sprang to the taffrail and shouted: "Bark *Betsey,* New Bedford. Western Ocean and South Seas. Three years."

"Gosh! Does he mean they're to be gone three years?" exclaimed Bob.

"I expect he does," replied his uncle. "Whaling cruises often last three or four years."

"What are all those boats for and what's that big gangway in her side?" inquired Harry.

"The boats are whaleboats,—used in capturing whales and the gangway is where they cut in the blubber on the grounds."

"On the 'grounds,'" repeated Harry. "I didn't know they caught whales from shore."

Mr. Bennet laughed and Captain Ned gave a loud guffaw.

"'Grounds' in whalemen's parlance means those parts of the sea where whales are liable to be found," explained his father. "But if you are interested in whaling, ask Captain Ned about it," he continued. "I know very little myself."

"Reckon I can't tell ye much," declared the Captain when the boys turned to him for further information. "All I knows is what I l'arned knockin' around New Bedford an' Nantucket. We're boun' fer New Bedford an' that's the spot fer ye to l'arn all about whales an' whalin'. They've got a museum there,—Old Dartmouth Historical S'ciety, I b'lieve they calls it,—what's chock-a-block with whalin' gear an' ye'll find a heap o' ol' whalemen at the Seamen's Home an' knockin' about town. They'll jes' enjiy spinnin' yarns fer ye."

"Well, I'm going there," declared Harry. "I mean to find out all there is to know about those ships and how they catch whales. Somehow, just thinking of that old bark going off for three

THE BOYS' BOOK OF WHALERS

years gave me a sort of thrill. I'll bet they have *some* adventures on their cruises."

"Reckon they do," agreed old Ned. "Ye'll find records o' a heap o' mutinies an' pirates an' wracks an' being stove in an' sech, over to the museum."

"I'll bet you could tell us some of those too," declared Bob. "Now, Cap'n Ned, be a good sport and tell us some whaling stories. We won't be in New Bedford for hours and there's nothing else to amuse us."

"Wall," replied the old sailor with a grin, "I 'spect I won't get no rest 'til I does, so I might jes' as well. But I ain't no whaleman, an' as I said afore, I don't know much about the game. When I was a kid, old New Bedford was jes' a whalin' town and not much else. Why, I recollec' the time when Merrill's wharf was that full o' bar'ls o' ile ye couldn' hardly see the mas'heads o' the ships 'longside. An' ships!— why, boys, I'm a-tellin' o' the Gospel truth when I says I've counted of nigh a hundred ships 'longside that ol' dock, an' all square-riggers too. Nowadays, 'less times have changed a lot sence I was here last, ye can't find a dozen altogether,

THE BOYS' BOOK OF WHALERS

an' them jes' o'nary Portugee schooners. But ye was askin' me fer to spin ye a yarn. Well, I reckon 'bout the bes' yarn I ever heard 'bout the whalers was 'bout a mut'ny aboard o' a Portugee schooner, the *Pedro Varela*,—like as not ye'll see her 'longside the docks to New Bedford—what was about the funniest sort o' mut'ny ever I heard on. 'Cordin' to the yarn, the *Varela* sailed with about as rotten a crew o' scallywags as ye could find an' 'bout six months arter they'd sailed all hands was jes' dog-tired o' whalin' an' pinin' for home an' the slums. Not bein' proper sailormen, an' a passel o' cowards, they didn't dare kill none o' the officers, but jes' decided to fix things so's the v'yage would have to end. Every night, the rascals on watch would heave overboard everything they could sot han's on. First thing 'twas the handspikes to the win'-lass; nex', the blubber-tackles an' carp'nter's tools; then the harpoons an' lances, 'til purty soon, there weren't nary a bit o' gear left. Even the grin'stone went, an' afore they knowed it, the cap'n found that even if they did raise a whale 'twouldn't do 'em a mite o' good cause they couldn't catch it. Course the skipper swore and

THE BOYS' BOOK OF WHALERS

threatened, but he might jes' as well saved his breath, 'cause nothin' he nor the crew could do'd bring the gear back from the bottom o' the sea. Fin'ly, seein' as how 'twasn't a mite o' use, the skipper claps the whole bunch in irons and sails off to the Azores. Jes' as luck would have it, a Yankee man-o'-war was in port an' the skipper o' the *Varela* turns his mut'neers over to the cruiser. Well, the long an' the short o' the matter was, that the gang was brought back to the States an' tried fer mut'ny, an' thet's where the funny part comes in. The jedge jes' couldn't convict 'em, 'cause 'cordin' to law, they hadn't committed no mut'ny. Hadn't refused to obey orders nor threatened nor attacked an officer, an' nary a officer could prove the crew had throwed the gear over the side. So all the Court done was to give 'em each ten days in jail fer a bit o' justice."

Both boys were highly amused at this story of a novel mutiny and begged the sailing-master for another yarn, until after a bit, he related the story of Marshall Jenkins, which is one of the most amazing adventures ever recorded in the annals of whaling.

THE BOYS' BOOK OF WHALERS

"This 'ere yarn was tol' to me by a ol' whaling cap'n who swore 'twas true," announced Captain Ned. "An' I reckon 'twas, 'cause I've met a lot o' chaps since what's heard the yarn an' one lad said he'd seen a ol' log in the museum with the same yarn in it. Well, 'cordin' to the story, long back in '70 this chap Jenkins went in on a sparm whale an' made a good strike with his iron,—that's the harpoon, ye know—but 'stead o' tearin' off with the boat in tow like they gen'rally does, this 'ere ol' whale jes' nat'rally got rip-roarin' mad, and turnin' round, snapped the boat in two, and grabbin' Jenkins in his jaws dove down to the bottom o' the sea,—'sounded,'—as the whalers say. Well, o' course his mates all thought Jenkins was gone to Davy Jones' locker all right, an' they clumb up on the two halves o' their boat a-waitin' for their ship to pick 'em up. They hadn't been there more'n a minute when up comes Mr. Whale right 'longside and spits Jenkins out an' plumb into the fore part o' the broken boat. An', by crickety, that chap weren't none the worse, 'ceptin' for a few bruises, and was back to whalin' again inside a fortni't!"

"My, that is a whopper!" exclaimed Harry.

THE BOYS' BOOK OF WHALERS

"You don't mean to say you expect us to believe that, do you?"

"It's quite true," declared Mr. Bennet, who had been listening to old Ned's story. "I saw the account of the marvelous incident in the original log. But here's New Bedford ahead, boys."

CHAPTER II

ALMOST the first thing that the boys did, after arriving in New Bedford, was to hunt up the Old Dartmouth Historical Society and its wonderful museum of whales and whalers. Here they found themselves in a new world and in the midst of most interesting and fascinating objects of which they had never dreamed. Here, in a special building, was a model of a famous whaler, complete in every detail and just one-half natural size. In another room was a whaleboat with all its gear just as it would be when the hardy whalemen were about to go after a whale. In cases and on shelves were a thousand and one objects used by whalers; models of their boats and appliances, ornaments and curios brought by them from far distant lands; handiwork of the men; harpoons, lances and other weapons; relics of famous ships; old logbooks and records, and paintings and pictures galore. It was all so wonderful and so confusing that, as Harry put it, the only way was to begin at the beginning. But then the question arose as to what and where the beginning was. Bob suggested that they begin with the oldest specimens, and while they were discussing this matter the genial curator approached and inquired if he could be of any service.

The boys at once told of their newly-aroused interests in whaling and their desire to learn all that they could of the industry while they were in New Bedford.

"There's an immense amount of detail to learn," said the curator. "But it's all very interesting and mighty important as well, although ninety people out of one hundred would not think so, and haven't the least idea that whaling, —if, in fact, they ever heard of it,—has any bearing on the history or progress of the United States. But, as a matter of fact, whaling has had a tremendous influence on our history, our commerce and our country."

"Well, we would like to begin at the very beginning and learn all we can," Harry assured him. "From what we've seen here we know it must be just full of interest, and we'd love to look over the old logs and read about the adventures the men had. Our sailing-master told us one or two stories he'd heard, and if they're all as good as those the logs must be as exciting as any book."

"I'll be very glad to tell you everything I can, and you're welcome to read the logs and old papers," replied the curator. "But if you want to start at the very beginning, and won't be bored, I'll first give you an outline of the early days of whaling and what it meant to the United States."

Assuring their new-found friend that nothing would please them more, the boys seated themselves at the curator's request and listened attentively to his story of the whalers.

"We owe the whalers a great deal," he began, "although few people realize the fact any more than they realize what a prominent part they took in the history and prosperity of the United States, the riches they brought or what an important part they played in the exploration, civilization and trade of the world. A whale ship was the first vessel to carry the Stars and Stripes into a British port, and the first time our flag was ever seen on the western coast of South

THE BOYS' BOOK OF WHALERS

America was when it was flown from a whaling ship's masthead. Long before any merchant ship or man-o'-war had carried Old Glory to far distant lands the flag was known to the natives through seeing it flaunted by the New England whalers. In many an unknown and uncharted island the savages first saw white men when a Nantucket or New Bedford whaler dropped anchor off their shores.

"Almost fifty years before the famous ride of Paul Revere the New England whalemen had explored and navigated Davis Straits, and within a dozen years after the Declaration of Independence, a Nantucket whaling ship,—the *Penelope* —had cruised farther north than was reached by any vessel for a hundred years thereafter. Years before Perry had opened Japan to the commerce of the world, whaling vessels had visited its shores and one whaleman had lived in Japan and had taught the natives English.

"It was Captain Folger, a Nantucket whaleman, who first discovered the flow and direction of the Gulf Stream, and it was from his rude sketches that Benjamin Franklin had a map made,—a map which revolutionized the commerce between Europe and America forever after. Brave to recklessness, accustomed daily to taking most fearful risks and to fighting against the mightiest creature in the world, splendid seamen and loving danger, the whalers often performed most marvelous feats of heroism and bravery for which they got no credit. It was the crews of two whaling vessels, from this little town of New Bedford, who saved the garrison of San José, California, in 1846. When the government buildings at Honolulu were burned it was whalemen who saved the town, and whenever a war broke out the stout-hearted, sturdy whalers were always prompt to enlist, and much of our success in famous old naval battles was due to the whalemen serving on American ships.

"I wish I could honestly tell you that all the whalemen were brave, noble-hearted, patriotic and honest men, but unfortunately there were all sorts and conditions of men among them as in every other trade or profession. Many of them were utterly mercenary and would undertake anything or commit any act no matter how brutal, dishonest or abominable it might be for the sake of money to be gained, and they drew the line at actual piracy only through fear of the consequences should their acts become known. As long as whales were to be had they usually stuck to whaling, as it was the trade they knew best and was the safest and surest in the end. But many of them saw far larger profits in less legitimate enterprises and chief among these was slaving. No one will ever know how many poor, miserable blacks were transported from Africa to be sold as slaves in the West Indies and South America on the oil-soaked, stinking whale ships. But it is certain, and a well-known historical fact, that many a New Bedford and New England fortune was made on the profits of slaving, although those who made the money were ostensibly whalers. It was a very easy matter for a whaler to start on a cruise, visit the African coast, carry a cargo of 'black ivory,' as the slaves were called, to the West Indies and then, after cruising on the whaling grounds, return with a cargo of oil. In the earlier days when slavery was recognized by nearly all nations this was of course looked upon as a perfectly honorable way of adding to a ship's profits and in later years, when slavery still existed but the exportation of slaves from Africa had been abolished or rather forbidden, it was still a most difficult and well-nigh impossible matter to prove that a whale ship had engaged in 'blackbirding' as it was called. The men, if they told, would not be believed and if they were it meant they would be held, if not as accessories as witnesses, and the class of men who shipped on whale ships had no desire to be held by the law even as witnesses and of course the whalemen never told of their own deeds when sober.

"Of all the slave ships the whalers were the worst and the conditions under which the negroes were brought across the sea were appalling and almost incredible. The real slavers were fast ships, their holds, though dark, ill ventilated or not ventilated at all, were at least roomy, their only cargo was slaves and the rascals who operated them had had experience in carrying slaves and to a certain extent knew how to care for them.

"Of course the agonies the poor blacks endured were awful. They were shackled in the foul hold with no sanitary arrangements, they

THE BOYS' BOOK OF WHALERS

were deathly sick, they were ill fed, they were sometimes kept below decks for days at a time if the weather were bad and if they sickened they were often tossed overboard to save the trouble of doctoring them or to avoid the spread of disease. But after all, it was to the slavers' interests to make the quickest possible runs. Every slave lost was so much money from their pockets and the more slaves they could bring to market and the better the condition in which they arrived the more they could demand for them. As a result, these true slavers did all they could, or knew how, to keep their human freight alive and in fairly good shape until the slave markets of Cuba and the West Indies were reached. Then, when the British and other nations proclaimed the slave trade illegal and proceeded to capture and sink every slaver they found these men were largely forced out of their nefarious trade. A pure out and out slaver was easily recognized and even if, as often happened, they were searched and no slaves found upon them, they were liable to seizure under suspicion. But with the whalers, conditions were very different and far worse. These ships were slow—they were built for seaworthiness and not speed, their holds reeked with whale oil, they were filled with casks and supplies for whaling, their officers knew nothing of handling slaves and as it was a side venture the captains and their crews looked upon it as a sort of gamble and cared very little whether or not they got their black ivory into port alive or in what condition. As a result, the miserable blacks that fell to the lot of a whaler slaver were lucky when they died. They were thrown into the reeking hold, packed in like sardines, shackled and uncared for. Only barely enough rotten water and wormy, mouldy food was given them to maintain life and each day all those who were too ill, weak or exhausted to stand were thrown to the sharks like so much garbage. If one-tenth of the original number of slaves survived the long passage the whalemen were satisfied, for the profits, especially after the trade was forbidden, were enormous. And if conditions were such when all went well, imagine what it was when a whaler engaged in the illicit trade was sighted by a man-of-war and was chased. Then the only way to save themselves was to leave no evidence on board

THE BOYS' BOOK OF WHALERS

and hurriedly the trembling, shuddering, moaning blacks were routed up, shackled together with heavy chains and thrown into the sea in groups. By the time the corvette arrived and the whale ship hove-to no evidence was there to prove slaves had ever been carried, and as a whaler might be anywhere on legitimate business and as there were always casks, gear and usually some oil aboard it was almost impossible to prove a case. As a result, nine-tenths of the whale ships that engaged in slaving went free, but many were taken, the captains and officers convicted and sentenced and the ships confiscated. It is one of the blackest pages in the history of New England and the worst of it is that it did not cease even when the hue and cry to abolish slavery in our Southern States went up. Even while our Northern people were rabidly denouncing slavery and 'Uncle Tom's Cabin' was inflaming the minds of New Englanders with the horrors of slavery, money contributed to the cause was being earned through transporting slaves on New England ships. Many a righteous deacon who publicly decried the sins and disgraces of our Southern planters for holding slaves was

THE BOYS' BOOK OF WHALERS

pocketing his share of the profits from running a cargo of black ivory into some South American port, and many a puritanical old New England family was being supported by the same nefarious business. No doubt many of the members of the whalemen's families were quite blameless and innocent of the source of the money they spent, for it is not likely that even the most calloused and hardened old reprobate of a whaler confided the secret of his successful and profitable voyages to his wife and family or even to his cronies, but nevertheless it was on the whole an open secret and many a whaleman boasted of his escape from men-o'-war and of getting slave cargoes into port.

"I do not know if any one can say when the last whaler carried a cargo of slaves, but that it continued to be a lucrative and not uncommon venture up to the time of the Civil War is easily proven. In the New Bedford Shipping List of December 3rd, 1861, appears the following:

"'SENTENCE OF SAMUEL P. SKINNER

"'In the U. S. Court in Boston on Friday, Judge Clifford sentenced Samuel P. Skinner, convicted of fitting out the Barque *Margaret Scott* of New Bedford for the slave trade, to pay a fine of one thousand dollars and to be confined at hard labor for a term of five years in the jail at Taunton.'

" In that same year another ship—the *Brutus* of New Bedford, fitted for a slave voyage and was successful in putting a cargo of 650 negroes ashore in Cuba. However, we may be thankful that her owners did not escape scot free, for one was convicted and sentenced to several years' imprisonment and the others were fined heavily. By that time, of course, every effort was being made to suppress the trade and scores of seized whaling ships were moored in Boston and other ports. And as a most fitting end to the careers of these ships and as a just retribution, the condemned vessels were loaded with stone, sent south and were sunk to blockade the Confederate ports.

"But I am getting a bit ahead of the beginning of whaling. Whaling began almost with the landing of the Pilgrims and Cape Cod was settled principally because whales were common in its waters. By 1639 one of the most important revenues of Massachusetts was from whaling, and within the next two years Long Island had been settled by whalers. The industry was so important to the colony that the town of Southampton was divided into four wards of eleven people each whose sole duty it was to secure and cut up the whales that came ashore. But at that time no whaling had been done from ships, all the whales being captured close to shore by means of small boats. In fact, it was not until 1688 that the first whaling ship, the brigantine *Happy Return,* sailed from Boston for the Bahamas and Florida on a search for sperm whales. But within a dozen years a fleet of hundreds of barks, brigs, schooners and sloops were engaged in the business and were scattered over the seven seas. As a result, many of the little coast towns and villages of New England were famous throughout the world, and in many a far-distant land, and to many a savage or strange race, the names of New Bedford, Gay Head, Nantucket, New London or Sag Harbor were more familiar than New York or Boston.

"But of all these ports New Bedford was the most famous as headquarters for the whalemen, and the town was practically built up and developed through whaling and the industries dependent upon it.

"And now, boys, before I begin to describe the whaling ships and the lives of the whalers, you must learn something about the various kinds of whales and their ways, for there were a great many different kinds of whaling, and for each sort of whale the methods, implements and weapons were specially designed.

"Perhaps you may think of whales as fish, and many old sailors and whalemen speak of them as such; but in reality whales, as well as their relatives the porpoises, dolphins and grampus, are warm-blooded mammals which bring forth their young alive and suckle them like any four-footed land mammal. Moreover, they breathe air and possess lungs and are obliged to rise frequently to the surface of the sea to 'spout' or 'blow' and it is their exhaled breath which forms the little puff of vapor which betrays the presence of whales to the whalemen. In fact, the ancestors of whales actually lived upon the land and the so-called 'fins' are really flippers or front legs adapted to a life in the sea, while the hind legs have been gradually lost, until now the only trace which remains are small bones completely hidden under the flesh.

"While there are a great many kinds of whales, only a few were hunted by the old New England whalemen, although nowadays, steam whaling ships, harpoon-guns and bomb-lances have made possible the capture of many kinds of whales which the old-time whalers did not consider worth while. The most important whales, to the New England whalemen, were the *sperm whales, bowheads* and *right whales,* but they also took the *finbacks, humpbacks* and *sulphur-bottom* whales, and when nothing else was available, they captured *grampuses, porpoises, white whales* and the *narwhal* or *unicorn whale.* Very often, too, they visited the remote islands of the Antarctic and South Indian Oceans and captured sea-elephants.

"Of all the whales the sperm whale and right whale were the most hunted as they were the most valuable; the sperm whale for its blubber, oil and the waxlike oily substance called 'spermaceti' contained in a cavity of the head, while the right whale provided oil and whalebone. Sperm whales are denizens of temperate and tropical seas, while the right whales and bowheads live in the Arctic and Antarctic waters, and while the two latter are really distinct, they are so much alike that a description of one will do for both. Although the oil of these whales was never as valuable as that of the sperm whales, yet the 'bone' or baleen was formerly about the most valuable of whaling products, and as a result the right whale and bowhead fisheries were among the largest and most important of the whaling industry. To the ordinary person, the most noticeable difference between the right whales and bowheads and the sperm whales is that the sperm whale has an enormous, square-ended head with the mouth near the lower side, while the bowheads and right whales have rounded heads with the mouth near the top. But really the greatest difference lies in the jaws and the manner of feeding. The lower jaw of the sperm whale is long, slender and pointed and is armed with many huge, sharp-pointed and strong teeth,—as you will see by examining the jaws in the other room,— whereas the right whales and bowheads, and, in fact, all other whales, possess no teeth, but have a curious horn-like material growing from the upper jaw in the form of a thick fringe. This is the so-called 'bone' and serves the whales as a strainer, for these creatures live upon tiny marine animals which they capture by filling their mouths with water and then closing their jaws and forcing the water out through the 'bone,' leaving all the small creatures that were in the water in the whale's mouth. The sperm whale, on the other hand, dives to the bottom of the sea and lives upon cuttlefish or squids which he bites to pieces with his sharp teeth. This difference in habits and structure of jaws makes a vast difference in the way the several varieties of whales were hunted. Thus, the right whales and bowheads cannot see ahead and cannot defend themselves with their jaws, while the sperm whales cannot see backwards and can easily bite a whaleboat in two with their powerful, armed jaws. Both kinds, however, can strike with their tails or flukes and do tremendous damage, although the right whale's tail is the far more dangerous of the two and can be swung from eye to eye. 'Beware of a right whale's flukes and a sperm whale's jaw,' is an old whalemen's maxim, and in hunting them the whalers were always careful to approach the sperm whale from the rear and the right whales and bowheads from in front.

"And just as there was a great deal of difference in the way that sperm whales and right whales were captured so, too, the methods used in cutting or stripping off the blubber or 'cutting in,' as it is called, varied according to the kind of whale.

"If you will go to the docks and examine any of the whale ships, or if you look at the model here in the museum, you will see a broad opening or gangway on the starboard side of every whaling vessel. This is the cutting-in gangway, and when a whale is alongside a ship a light, flimsy platform, known as the 'cutting stage,' is swung out from the ship's side below this gangway. The men standing on this cut the blubber or fat from the whale's carcass by means of sharp-edged 'spades' on long handles. As soon as the whale 'spouted blood' or was killed, a chain was passed around its flukes, or tail, and it was towed to the ship. But you must not think for a moment that it was an easy job to do this. In fact, it was an undertaking of tremendous risk and danger, except in the smoothest weather. Very often night fell before the whale was killed, and still oftener, the seas ran high and the wind blew half a gale. Then, with the huge dead whale wallowing in the sea and as dangerous to the tiny boats as an island, the whalemen required all their skill and courage and strength to get the towing-chain about the root or 'small' of the huge tail or flukes. If two or more boats were at hand it was not so bad, for by passing a light, weighted line under the flukes, and then drawing a heavier rope and finally a chain, by this, the operation could be accomplished without much danger, but if only one boat was present,—as was more often the case,—the difficulties to be overcome were almost incredible. Only by a man standing on, or holding to, the dead whale was it possible to pass the rope and chain under and around the whale's flukes. Secured by a rope about his waist, one of the daring men would climb upon the slippery whale and, while alternately buried in the tumbling seas and forced to cling for his life to the whale, he would finally get the line in place. Very often, too, the whale would be killed miles away from the ship, and after a hard day's work, the men would be obliged to tow the mountain of flesh and blubber through a rough sea and against a head wind for hours.

"Then, when it is at last alongside, the dirtiest and hardest work of all begins. First a hole is cut through the blubber between the eye and the fin, and in this a huge hook is placed which is attached to a heavy tackle led from the ship's mast. Then cuts are made through the blubber at each side with a cross-cut connecting them, and by hoisting away on the hook the strip of blubber is stripped from the whale's body, and in so doing the carcass is rolled over on its side. Next, if the catch is a sperm whale, a cut is made between the upper jaw and the mass of blubber above, and which is known as the 'junk,' and if the whale is very large a cut is also made between the junk and the upper portion of the head known as the 'case.' A cut is also made across the root of the lower jaw at the corner of the mouth, a chain is fastened to the jaw and as this is raised by one tackle the other is slacked off until the whale lies upon its back. The men then cut through the end of the tongue and the flesh and the jaw are hoisted to the deck. Then, by turning the body over by means of the tackles, cuts are made in the junk to which straps and lines are fastened and the tackles heaved up until the body is nearly vertical, when the men cut the immense head free from the body and moor it to the ship's quarter while they proceed to strip off the blubber. This is done by cutting spirally around the body and hauling on the tackles so that the great strip, or 'blanket-piece,' is pulled off or unrolled until the flukes are reached, when it is cut off and hoisted on deck. The head is then hauled to the gangway, and either hoisted bodily on deck in the case of a small whale, or separated into the junk and case, the former being taken aboard and the latter lifted to the deck level and a hole cut in and the spermaceti baled out, or if the whole head is taken aboard the spermaceti is baled out on deck. When first taken from the case, this valuable material is liquid and oil-like but it rapidly hardens upon exposure to the air.

"Meanwhile, the blubber, or blanket-piece, is

BEFORE LONG THE LAST OLD YANKEE WHALE SHIP WILL BE BUT A MEMORY OF THE PAST

WHEN THE WHALE IS AT LAST ALONGSIDE THE DIRTIEST AND HARDEST WORK OF ALL BEGINS

lowered into the hatch and stowed skin-side down, in the blubber-room, where it is hacked into pieces about a foot square, which are taken on deck to the mincing-horse to be chopped up by big, two-handled mincing knives or by a machine. The minced chunks of blubber are then placed in huge iron kettles and boiled on the try works—brick fireplaces near the foremast,—by fires fed by the blubber from which the oil has been boiled out and known as 'cracklings.' As fast as the oil is boiled from the minced blubber it is ladled into a cooler and then into casks which are finally headed up and stored below decks. At last, when all of the blanket-piece has been tried out, the junk is cut up and boiled separately, as the oil from this is of superior quality and commands a very high price. All that I have told you relates to the cutting in of a sperm whale, but if the catch is a right whale or bowhead the entire head is not taken aboard, the valuable whalebone only being saved.

"All this cutting in and boiling is the most exhausting, back-breaking work which the whalemen are compelled to perform, and there is no lull or let-up in the ceaseless toil for three or four days while boiling is going on. The work is divided into watches of six hours,—and here it may be well to remember that whaling ships always keep six bell watches instead of eight bell watches like merchantmen, or, in other words, the watches on a whaler are from 7 until 11 A. M., from 11 until 3, and from 3 until 7, instead of from 8 to 12, from 12 to 4 and from 4 to 8. Moreover, the whalers never ring the half hours on the bells. While cutting and boiling, half the crew is constantly at work with the officers, such as mates and boat-steerers, looking after the fires and ladling out the oil, while one man is always at the wheel and another is constantly at the lookout at the masthead.

"But if cutting in and boiling is the hardest work and is unspeakably dirty and nauseating, it is nothing as compared with the casks of 'fat lean' in point of filth and odor. Fat leans are the parts of the blubber which have bits of meat attached to them, and as these cannot readily be boiled down, they are tossed into open casks to rot for the sake of the oil which drains from them. When the mass has thoroughly decomposed the men are compelled to lean inside the casks and fish out the putrid meat with their hands while breathing the awful fumes and terrific stench for hours at a time.

"There is an old saying that one can smell a whale ship twenty miles to windward, and this is scarcely exaggeration. How any human beings could stand the life of hard work, danger, poor food, years at sea, awful smells and incredible filth is something the ordinary mortal cannot understand.

"Now, boys, I've given you an idea of the worst part of whaling, and if you'll come around to-morrow I'll tell you about the ships in which these hardy men went to sea, the manner of men they were and how the whales were caught."

CHAPTER III

"YOU can understand," said the curator, when the boys visited his office the following day, "that vessels which were intended to withstand the gales and seas of every ocean for years at a time had to be the strongest, staunchest, most seaworthy and able ships which man could build. For month after month they cruised beneath the scorching equatorial sun, while the pitch bubbled from their deck seams and the woodwork dried and warped; then, for months, or even years, they were buffeted by Arctic gales, nipped in ice-floes, frozen fast for the long, dreary months of Polar winters, and a few months later would be scudding under bare poles before an East Indian typhoon. Often, at the end of a three or four years' voyage, they would be stripped and laid up on the mud flats, neglected and forgotten, until weeds and grass sprouted from their opening seams, and then,

THE BOYS' BOOK OF WHALERS

years later, they would be patched up, refitted and once again would sail, to cruise far and near upon the stormiest parts of all the oceans. To the whalemen, seaworthiness was everything, and speed, comfort and appearance were of no importance, and while no stronger, better ships were ever built, yet most of them were heavy, bluff-bowed and tubby. Of course there were some which were models of beauty,—as graceful and swift as the famous old clippers, and many of the captains kept their ships as spick and span, as well painted, as clean, and with rigging as taut and well tarred as any yacht. But the bulk of the ships, even if they sailed forth trim and neat, returned, dingy, weather-beaten, scarred with innumerable battles of the sea and ice and so thoroughly soaked with grease and oil that their planks could have been boiled out in a try works. And often, when a ship returned from a long cruise, she looked more like the *Flying Dutchman* or a derelict than like a real ship. But the whalemen were out for oil and to make money and had enough to occupy hands and minds without spending time keeping their ships in order. Between catching, cutting, boiling and necessary work, the men had no time to devote to keeping their vessels in trim and only did the most essential things to keep the ships afloat and seaworthy. Always there were smashed boats to be repaired, lines and ropes to be spliced, harpoons or 'irons' to be made, tools to be sharpened, iron poles to be made and fitted and the men's work was so hard, so dangerous and so exhausting while capturing the whales, cutting-in and boiling that both officers and men were compelled to rest between whiles in order to be fit for the next chase. For this reason the crews were never compelled to do other than absolutely necessary duties aboard ship and were allowed to amuse themselves in any way they saw fit. Many of them were adepts at carving bone and whales' teeth and devoted days and weeks to engraving the teeth of sperm whales, or 'scrimshawing' as it's called, or making chessmen, ornaments and other curios from the teeth or bones of the whales they killed. In scrimshawing teeth the design was first scratched upon the smooth surface of the tooth and then colors, such as paint, India ink or soot, were rubbed into the lines, the result resembling a steel engraving printed on the tooth. And many of these scrimshawed teeth, although made only with a sailor's knife, were as fine, as artistic and as beautiful as any etching or engraving. Sometimes the men designed their own pictures, but the best were traced or transferred from book illustrations or magazines. Many of the other articles they made were also marvels of patience and skill, for time was of no account and hung heavy on the men's hands. Their cribbage-boards, made from walrus tusks, their ivory chessmen, their inlaid table tops, boxes and other articles of bone, tortoise-shell and mother-of-pearl, were as delicate and well-finished as anything produced by the artisans of the Orient. But perhaps the happiest hours of the whalemen's lives when at sea were when they met another ship and all went 'gamming,' or visiting. There were letters to be sent home and received, news from home and distant ports to be heard, comparisons of catches made, and plenty of liquor to be drunk, tobacco to be smoked and chewed and specially good food to be eaten, for to 'gam' was to have a real celebration in forecastles as well as in the cabins. At such times the men would strive to outdo one another in yarns and stories and in boasting of their catches and oil; they danced and skylarked on the decks; they held boat races; those who had battered fiddles or concertinas brought them out, and to the music the whalemen sang their songs and chanteys, many of which were sentimental, others descriptive of their lives, others merely rollicking lays; but all bearing on the men's occupation, their hopes, fears or sufferings, the dangers that they faced or their desire to see home once more. One favorite song was this:

" ' 'Twas advertised in Boston,
    New York and Buffalo,
Five hundred brave Americans,
    A-whaling for to go.

They send you to New Bedford,
    The famous whaling port;
They send you to a shark's store,
    And board and fit you out.

They send you to a boarding-house,
    For a time to dwell;
The thieves there, they are thicker
    Than the other side of hell.

THE BOYS' BOOK OF WHALERS

They tell you of the whaling ships,
   A-going in and out;
They swear you'll make your fortune
   Before you're five months out.

But now we're out at sea, my boys,
   We find life hard enough;
A little piece of stinking meat
   And a darned small bag of duff.

Next comes the running rigging,
   Which you're all supposed to know;
'Tis "Lay aloft, you son-of-a-gun,
   Or overboard you go."

The cap'n's on the quarter-deck,
   A-squintin' at the sails,
Aloft four men are standin',
   A-searchin' for sperm whales.

The cooper at his vise bench
   Is makin' iron-poles,
And the mate upon the main hatch
   Is cursin' all our souls.'

"Or again, some jolly, rollicking, hearty song would be roared out by a score of lusty lungs, like the following:

"'We're homeward bound, oh, happy sound!
   Good-bye, fare ye well,
   Good-bye, fare ye well!
Come, rally the crew and run quick around,
Hurrah, my bullies, we're homeward bound!

Our yards we'll swing and our sails we'll set,
   Good-bye, fare ye well,
   Good-bye, fare ye well!
The whales we are leaving, we leave with regret,
Hurrah, my bullies, we're homeward bound!

Oh, heave with a will and heave long and strong,
   Good-bye, fare ye well,
   Good-bye, fare ye well!
Oh, sing a good chorus, for 'tis a good song,
Hurrah, my bullies, we're homeward bound!

We're homeward bound at last, they say,
   Good-bye, fare ye well,
   Good-bye, fare ye well!
Then tail on the braces and run her away,
Hurrah, my bullies, we're homeward bound!

We're homeward bound, may the winds blow fair,
   Good-bye, fare ye well,
   Good-bye, fare ye well!
Wafting us true to the friends waiting there,
Hurrah, my bullies, we're homeward bound!'

THE BOYS' BOOK OF WHALERS

"And in addition to their songs, which were strictly whaling songs, the Yankee whalemen had their chanteys as did the merchant sailors. Most of these were, in fact, identical with those sung on merchant ships, but many were altered to suit the needs or tastes of the whalemen. There was the famous halliard chantey of 'Whiskey Johnny':

> "'Oh, whiskey is the life of man,
>   Whiskey! Johnny!
> It always was since time began,
>   Oh, whiskey for my Johnny!
>
> Oh, whiskey makes me wear old clo's,
>   Whiskey! Johnny!
> 'Twas whiskey gave me a broken nose,
>   Oh, whiskey for my Johnny!
>
> A glass of grog for every man,
>   Whiskey! Johnny!
> And a bottle full for the Chantey Man,
>   Oh, whiskey for my Johnny!'

"Then there were the topsail chanteys, for each and every chantey had its use, and there were halliard chanteys, sheet, tack and bowline chanteys, capstan chanteys, and, in fact, chanteys to accompany every sort of work performed aboard the ships. A favorite topsail chantey was 'Hanging Johnny,' which ran:

> "'They call me Hanging Johnny,
>   Away-e-Oh!
> They call me Hanging Johnny,
>   So hang, boys, hang.'

"Then there was 'Cape Horn':

> "'I wish to the Lord I'd never been born,
>   To me way,—hay, hay,—yah!
> To go sailing round and round Cape Horn,
>   A long time ago—!
>
> Around Cape Horn where wild gales blow,
>   To me way,—hay, hay,—yah!
> Around Cape Horn through sleet and snow,
>   A long time ago—!
>
> Around Cape Horn with frozen sails,
>   To me way,—hay, hay,—yah!
> Around Cape Horn to hunt for whales,
>   A long time ago—!'

"Another favorite with the whalemen was 'Sally Brown,' and probably no old chantey has ever spread so far and wide as this. Wherever one goes,—to the distant South Sea Islands, to

the spice-laden Caribbees, to the frozen shores of
Alaska or Hudson's Bay,—one will hear the air
and words, often mutilated and mispronounced,
but always recognizable. It's a long chantey,
but the first verse is:

> " 'Oh, Sally Brown of New York City,
>   Aye Sally,—Sally Brown,
> Of pretty Sal this is a ditty,
>   I'll spend my money on Sally Brown!'

"Some of the chanteys, too, were meaningless
and ridiculous jumbles of words, such as the one
which began:

" 'There once was a ship in the northern sea,
   And the name of the ship was the *Green
     Willow Tree*,
As we sailed in the lowlands, lies so low,
And oh, we sailed in the lowlands O,'

while others were really humorous, such as the
one that commenced:

> " 'Oh, the jackass is a pretty bird,
>   He is so neat and slick,
> One-half of him is head and ears,
>   The other half is kick!'

"Or again, this one:

"'And who d'ye think's the skipper o' her?
Blow, boys, blow!
Why, Holy Joe, the nigger lover!
Blow, my bully boys, blow!

Now who d'ye think's the chief mate o' her?
Blow, boys, blow!
A big mul-latter come from Antigua!
Blow, my bully boys, blow!

And what d'ye think we had for dinner?
Blow, boys, blow!
Mosquito's heart and sandfly's liver,
Blow, my bully boys, blow!'

"But perhaps the greatest favorite among the whalemen, as it was the most appropriate, was the capstan chantey known as 'Fishes':

"'Oh, a ship she was rigged and ready for sea,
Windy weather! Stormy weather!
And all of her sailors were fishes to be,
Blow ye winds westerly, gentle sou'westerly,
Blow ye winds westerly,—steady she goes.

Oh, first came the herring, the king o' the sea,
Windy weather! Stormy weather!
He jumped on the poop. "I'll be cap'n!" cried he.

THE BOYS' BOOK OF WHALERS

Blow ye winds westerly, gentle sou'westerly,
Blow ye winds westerly,—steady she goes.

Oh, next came a flatfish,—they call him a skate,
Windy weather! Stormy weather!
"If you be the cap'n why sure I'm the mate!"
Blow ye winds westerly, gentle sou'westerly,
Blow ye winds westerly,—steady she goes.'

" It was by singing such songs as these that the crew gave vent to their feelings and voiced their opinions of their officers, for, strange as it may seem, almost anything could be said or sung in a chantey without bringing reprimand or punishment, and the leader of the chanteys or the Chantey Man, as he was called, was a highly-privileged character and a great favorite on board ship. There is nothing in the world like a rousing song to help make hard work light, and the rhythm and cadence of the chanteys also enabled the men to pull or haul in unison and to labor to better advantage. This was appreciated by men and officers alike, and the chantey man, as a result, held a unique position and did little more than sing his way along, for his songs put such life and pep into the crew that officers would overlook his ' sojering ' tendencies.

"Usually the chantey man was an old hand who knew every song of the seven seas and the five oceans, and, in addition, he would improvise new ones or would add new verses or words to the old ones to suit the needs of the case or to express the feelings of himself and his mates in regard to officers, ship or work. Even the most brutal skippers and hardest down-east 'bucko' mates would grin good-naturedly at the vivid descriptions and pointed quips at their personalities and characters when roared forth in a chantey, although the same sentiments, if spoken, would have resulted in a knock-out blow with a belaying pin or worse.

"And now, perhaps, you may wonder what manner of men these were who sailed forth in the staunch old New England ships to battle with the elements and wage war with the giants of the deep for years on end.

"Many people imagine that the whalemen were seamen, and many songs and stories describe them as 'sailors' par excellence. As a matter of fact, however, the rank and file of whalemen were neither seamen nor sailors.

"To be sure, the captains, mates and 'boat-steerers' or harpooniers were among the best seamen the world has ever known, but the crews,— the men who did the hard work, pulled the boats, cut-in and boiled down the blubber and took all the knocks and blows,—were raw, rough landsmen of the worst type and were known as 'greenies.'

"Although there were plenty of good sailors in the New England ports, the whaling captains would have none of them and avoided the seamen as if they had the plague. Never, willingly, would they allow one on their ships, and, as one old captain put it, they wouldn't ship a sailor if he paid his passage.

"This may seem very strange, but the reason is simple. In the first place, your true deep-water sailor is a born grumbler and 'sea-lawyer' and he knows just how far his officers can carry bullying and abuse, what he is entitled to, the duties he must perform, and every custom and rule of the sea. He could not be fooled into shipping under the conditions that prevailed on whaling ships; he could not be induced to ship for 'lays,' or shares, in the catch, as did the whalemen, and if conditions did not suit him, he would desert at the first chance, and while at sea, would stir up discontent among the crew and would hatch out mutinies.

"For these reasons, the whaling ships drew their crews from the worst type of landsmen; riff-raff from far and near; gutter sweepings from the big cities, loafers from park benches; absconders and embezzlers; drunkards and ex-convicts, with a good sprinkling of discontented farm-hands, factory workers, ne'er-do-wells and men from the Middle West and interior States. These were attracted to the whaling ports by attractive, alluring posters and hand-bills advertising for men to go a-whaling and promising tremendous profits and a life of adventure and travel. Lured by these, the poor fellows gathered at the ports and entered their names on the shipping agent's or 'shark's' lists. In the advertisements the men were promised a lay[1] of

---

[1] The whalemen always worked for lays instead of wages. A lay being one barrel, or rather its value, of oil out of a definite number. The captain and officers had the largest lays, the coopers the next largest, the boat-steerers next, followed by the stewards, cooks, seamen and last of all the greenhands who received the smallest lays of all.
The exact division of the lays varied according to the ship, the time, the cruise and various other matters, but the following example of the division of lays, the amounts received and the catch taken will serve as an illustration.

the ship's catch,—in other words one barrel of oil out of a certain number,—an advance of seventy-five dollars, an outfit of clothes, board and lodging until aboard ship and good food. For each man obtained by these methods, the shipping agent was paid ten dollars and a refund for all expenses incidental to the transportation, board and outfit of the men, and as this was not to be paid until the men were on the ship, the sharks saw to it that the crew was on hand when the anchor was weighed.

"But the deluded men saw little come of the promises made to them. From the advance of

LAYS OF A NEW BEDFORD SHIP IN 1860

Dr.			Dr.	Lays	Value of lays
Amount of charge		$1,568.90	Captain	1/12	$3,258.34
Sundries		365.10	Mate	1/18	2,172.23
		$1,934.00	2nd Mate	1/28	1,396.44
Cr.			3d Mate	1/35	1,117.14
60,154 gals. oil		$39,100.10	Cooper	1/60	651.67
Due to ship		$21,606.49	10 Seamen each	1/150	2,606.70
Charge		1,934.00	13 Greenhands each	1/175	2,904.53
Bal. to owners		$19,672.49	4th Mate	1/60	651.67
			4 Boat-steerers each	1/80	1,955.00
			Steward	1/90	434.44
			Cook	1/110	355.45
					$17,493.61

seventy-five dollars were deducted all the expenses which the agents had paid out for the men, —as well as his ten-dollar fee,—and the prices he paid for every item of outfit were trebled or quadrupled; the train fares were doubled, the charges for the foul boarding-places where the men were housed were falsified, and when at last the bills were handed to the recruit and 'signed off' by him, he found he hadn't a cent to his name and was more frequently heavily in debt.

"No sailor could ever be bamboozled into this sort of thing unless he were drunk, and only the greenest of greenies, or men who had absolutely no other future, could be induced to submit to it. Moreover, the men thus secured knew so little of the sea and of foreign lands that they dared not desert, even if they had the chance, while there was no coöperation or organization among them, and therefore little danger of mutiny. To-day, however, this class of men is almost a thing of the past, and the whaling crews are made up largely of Portuguese from the Azores or Cape Verde Islands. Many of them are negroes, but nearly all are hard-working, skillful whalemen and willing to work and slave for returns which would not attract any white man. They have been at the whaling game for so long that they cannot be fooled, robbed or cheated by the 'sharks.' Even a great many of the captains of the modern whaling ships are Portuguese, and when whaling was on the decline and oil fell to such low prices that the ships were laid up and the industry nearly died, these men still made it a business and built fortunes from the whales which they chased and killed in their trim schooners, for they are satisfied with small profits, they can live cheaply and are very thrifty, even though they are never the splendid seamen that their Yankee predecessors were.

"Perhaps you may think that crews of men such as I have described would make poor whalemen, but this was not the case. Although many never learned to be seamen, and could not be taught, cursed or beaten into learning the various ropes and rigging of a ship, yet they developed a wonderful hardihood, courage and capacity for work and could handle the whaleboats to perfection.

"These boats, by the way, are the most seaworthy and safest small boats which were ever designed or built, and when properly handled can live in almost any sea. They are thirty feet long, six feet wide, and with a depth of twenty-two inches amidships and thirty-seven inches at bow and stern,—mere cockleshells in size,—but staunch, seagoing craft in the hands of the whalemen. They are rowed by five immense ash oars,—fourteen, sixteen and eighteen feet long, and are steered by a still longer twenty-two foot oar. On one side, are the sixteen-foot oars—known as the tub and bow oars—while on the opposite side are the fourteen-foot harpoonier's and after oars and the midship oar.

"Just as perfect for their purpose as the boats themselves is their equipment with every article designed for a specific purpose and always in its place, for an instant's delay or confusion or an article misplaced might mean death to all on board. On the sides at the bow are the irons or harpoons and the lances with their tips sheathed and resting in cleats all ready to be seized and used at a second's notice. Coiled in wooden tubs are the lines to hold the whales when struck—the finest hemp rope that can be made and three hundred fathoms in length. In

HER DINGY PATCHED SAILS WERE BELLYING OUT LIKE DUN-COLORED BALLOONS

THESE BOATS ARE THE MOST SEAWORTHY AND SAFEST SMALL BOATS WHICH WERE EVER DESIGNED OR BUILT

the bow-box is a hatchet, ready to cut the lines in case the whale 'sounds' and goes beyond the limit of the rope or in case it kinks or is jammed. There are candles, compasses, lanterns, glasses, matches and other articles in the stern locker. A keg of water is always in place as are boat-hooks, waif-flags, fluke-spades and buckets of canvas, and in addition, there are short paddles which are used in place of the oars when it is necessary to approach a whale cautiously and in silence.

"At the stem of the boat is a slot or 'chock' through which the line is led when the whale is 'fast,' and in the stern is a strong post known as a 'loggerhead,' over which a turn of the line is taken to hold it when being towed by the stricken whale. To prevent any noise, the rowlocks are covered, or 'thummed,' with greased marline, and in the front seat or thwart is a knee-brace called a 'clumsy cleat,' so that the whaleman may brace himself with his leg when throwing the harpoon or 'iron' at the whale.

"Most people think of the harpoons as light, spear-like affairs which are thrown like javelins at the whales; but in reality, they are immense, heavy weapons which must be held in both hands and heaved, and their extreme range is only about fifteen feet. Nowadays harpoons fired by guns with powder have largely taken the place of the old-time hand weapons; but many whalemen still prefer the old-fashioned implements. These harpoons, or 'irons,' are merely to capture the whale or make 'fast' until the creature is tired out and exhausted when he is killed by means of keen-bladed lances, or at the present time, more often by explosive bomb-lances.

"And now, having considered the ships, the boats, the men, and the weapons they used, let us accompany the whalemen to sea and learn how they lived and fared, how they fought and captured the whales and the adventures they had on their long voyages."

CHAPTER IV

"EVEN after a whale ship was ready for sea, after she had been 'hove-down'—or, in other words, pulled over on her side by tackles until her bottom was exposed,—cleaned, caulked and coppered; after her topsides had been repaired and painted, her rigging tarred down, renewed and tightened, her spars scraped and in place, when new sails had been bent on and from stem to stern, from truck to keel, she was ready for her long cruise,—there was still much to be done. First, there were the whaleboats and their equipment which I have already described. The number of these carried varied with the size of the vessel, but if a 'four-boat' ship, three were hung to the huge wooden davits on the port side and one on the quarter of the starboard side, as the big cutting-in gangway must be left clear. In addition, two or more extra boats were stored on overhead racks between the main and mizzen masts.

THE BOYS' BOOK OF WHALERS

"And then came the supplies, fittings, provisions and other articles which totaled over 650 different articles. By the time that these were aboard there was little room to spare, for every available inch of space was filled and the vessel became a floating warehouse, as well as a blacksmith shop, store, carpenter's shop, sail loft and ship chandlery. As the ships cruised mainly in the open ocean and were gone for years and seldom touched at any civilized ports, it was essential that they carry everything that might be needed for consumption, for use or for making repairs to the boats or the vessel herself. And when, at last, the ship set sail she was independent of the rest of the world and fully prepared to cope with any emergency which might arise.

"Aft were the officers' cabins and in the forecastle the crew lived. Rigging, hawsers, cutting-in gear and tackle; oars, anchors, lumber, and many other articles were packed in the forehold, while the main hold was filled with the casks destined to hold the oil, but which, when the ship set sail, were filled with provisions, supplies and fresh water. Those lowest down were filled with water, above these were casks containing food and a vast variety of miscellaneous articles, and on top, were those holding the goods which would be used before the first whales were taken, by which time they would be empty and ready to be filled with the precious oil.

"When we consider that every ship carried such a vast amount of stores, and that in the heyday of whaling, sixty ships or more sailed each season from New Bedford, with many more from Nantucket, Provincetown, Sag Harbor, Salem, Essex, Portland, New London and other ports, you can understand what the whaling business meant to New England.

"The stores alone for the New Bedford fleet amounted to two million dollars each season, while many millions more were expended for labor, for ship and boat building, for rigging, for boats, for spars, for sails and for the thousand and one other things which made whaling possible.

Some idea of the vast quantities of supplies required for outfitting the whale ships may be gained by the following list of supplies which were furnished in 1858 to the New Bedford fleet consisting of sixty-five vessels.

33,000 tons rivets	130,000 lbs. tobacco
450 whaleboats	5,200 lbs. linseed oil

"Thousands of workmen, skilled artizans and manufacturers were kept constantly at work, all dependent upon the whalers, and whale oil literally was king in those days, for life, commerce and business were all maintained and kept prosperous by the whaling fleets. Wherever there were forests, sawmills were built and the trees cut to furnish lumber for planks, timbers, barrels and cordwood. Many sail-lofts and rope-walks made nothing save cordage and sails for the whale ships. Scores of blacksmith shops and

23,000 bricks
2,000 candles
1,000 tons hoop iron
36,000 ft. oars
13,000 lbs. cotton twine
2,600 gals. rum
260 cords pine wood
15,000 lbs. sheath nails
65,000 ft. pine boards
205,000 yds. canvas
1,200 cords oak wood
520,000 lbs. copper
739,000 lbs. cordage
22,500 lbs. flags
234,000 yds. cotton cloth
39,000 gals. white lead
400 gals. turpentine
1,000 gals. liquors
260,000 ft. heading
400 bbls. tar
8,500 iron poles
1,000,000 staves
52,000 lbs. copper nails
32,500 ft. boat boards
200 casks lime

13,000 lbs. paint
120 casks powder
32,500 bbls. water
7,150 bbls. pork
78,000 lbs. sugar
14,300 lbs. tea
13,650 bbls. flour
39,000 lbs. rice
16,300 lbs. ham
26,000 bus. potatoes
97,500 gals. molasses
78,000 lbs. butter
1,950 bus. corn
10,400 bbls. beef
39,000 bbls. apples
18,000 lbs. coffee
400 bbls. vinegar
260 bbls. meal
13,000 bus. beans
32,500 lbs. codfish
1,300 bus. onions
19,500 bus. salt
19,500 lbs. cheese
13,300 lbs. raisins

THE BOYS' BOOK OF WHALERS

hundreds of smiths were kept busy from morn till night making lances, irons, blubber hooks and fittings, and boat yards near every whaling port turned out nothing but the staunch whaleboats. Spinning mills and textile factories were given over completely to turning out sailcloth, bunting and cotton for the whalemen's use. Whole farms sold their entire crops to supply the whalers and herds of cattle were required to supply the butter, cheese and beef. Cooperage shops by hundreds produced the thousands of casks and barrels required and there even were newspapers and periodicals devoted entirely to whaling and in which no word or line was printed which was not of interest to the whalemen or their families.

"And all these workers; these toilers; these experts, took a great pride and a personal interest in their work, for each and every one knew that upon the quality of his product depended in greater or less degree the success of the whalers, the size of the catches and even the lives of his neighbors. And, as a result, only work of the highest class, articles as near perfection as could be made, were good enough for the whalemen.

The rope makers realized that if their lines gave way the wounded whale would escape. The boat-makers knew that upon the staunchness, buoyancy and strength of their boats depended the success of the chase and the lives of the crew. Upon the temper of the blacksmith's steel hung the success of the harpoonier and the death of the whale. The sail-makers knew that the whale ship's sails must withstand months of tropic rains, weeks of scorching sun, ice-laden gales and clinging sleet, and the coopers strove to produce casks that would withstand the roughest usage and still stay tight and strong and hold the precious oil for months and years.

"When the last cask and box and bale was aboard, and when the boats had been swung in their places the ship waited only for its crew and officers. The average whaling ship carried a total of thirty-five to forty men. There were four boats' crews of four men each, or sixteen seamen; four ship-keepers or 'spare-men'; four boat-steerers; the captain or skipper; four 'officers' or mates; the cooper, the steward, the cook and one or more boys.

"Every man had his duties and his place and

was ready to do his part without hesitation. Each mate had a boat under his charge, while the captain often lowered also and went after whales himself. In each boat, too, in addition to the mate and the crew of four men, was a boat-steerer and every man in a boat was assigned to a certain place and to certain work. The first, or bow, oar was always the place of honor and the bow oarsman assisted the mate with his lances when killing a whale and was his right-hand man. The man who handled the long, heavy, midship oar, on the other hand, had little to do save pull on his oar while the tub oarsman's duty was to throw water on the line as it flew through the bow-chock when the whale dove or 'sounded' and the stroke-oarsman gave the time or 'strokes' to the others and also helped the boat-steerer in keeping a clear line and in hauling in and coiling it down.

"When the boat was approaching or 'going on' a whale, the first or 'harpoonier's' oar was pulled by the boat-steerer while the mate steered; but as soon as the whale was close, the boat-steerer threw the iron and struck the whale. Then, as soon as the boat was 'fast,' the mate went forward and the boat-steerer took his place at the steering oar while the mate stood in the bow and waited for his chance to kill the creature with the lance.

"Whenever the boats were lowered, the ship was left under short sail in charge of the captain (unless he took one of the boats), the four sparemen, the steward, cook, boys and cooper. Except when on the whaling grounds the seamen had little to do, for it was the best policy to let them rest and conserve their strength for the chase of the whale.

"I have already mentioned that the whalemen's watches were 'six bell' watches and moreover, when on the grounds, each boat's crew formed a watch thus giving four watches of three hours each for the night, that is if the vessel were a four-boat ship.

"Before darkness fell, the lighter sails were furled, the topsails reefed and the vessel was hove-to in the wind so that she would remain practically motionless, and by wearing ship now and again, the crew would find themselves at almost the same spot in the morning as on the preceding night. In the Arctic and Antarctic regions, however, whaling operations were continuous for there was no darkness and the whalemen made every hour count during their short seasons.

"Throughout the day, four lookouts were constantly kept on watch at the mastheads, two men being stationed forward, with a boat-steerer and mate aft, and on the grounds the ship would cover practically every square mile of the sea by taking long tacks to windward and then sailing down before the wind.

"All this, however, took place after the ship had been several weeks or months at sea and during the intervening time the life of the men was one incessant round of hard toil and labor. There were various odds and ends of cargo and stores to be stowed away, decks to be scoured or holy-stoned, gear to be overhauled and put in readiness for the chase and last, but most important of all, the 'greenies' had to be broken in.

"The bulk of the crew had never been to sea and knew nothing of ships, and not until the land was dropped well astern and the long cruise began did the poor, deluded landlubbers realize what was in store for them. But just as soon as the ship was 'out of soundings' or on the high seas their training or breaking in commenced. Although they might be, and usually were, deathly seasick and were filled with mortal terror of the lurching, rolling ship and grew dizzy almost to fainting whenever they looked up at the swaying, soaring masts, yet they were ordered into the rigging and compelled to go aloft. If they demurred or hesitated, they were spurred on by curses, kicks or blows, and as even the danger of going up the ratlines was preferable to the marline spike or ropes'-end held by the mate the poor fellows usually managed to crawl a few feet above the deck. In fact it was a case of necessity, for it would take a brave and courageous man indeed, to refuse to obey the orders of the hard-fisted, cursing mates, and the scums of humanity which formed the whaling crews were neither brave nor courageous. There is an old saying to the effect that 'needs must when the devil drives,' and the devil himself would have had no chance in a competition with a Yankee whaler's mate when it came to driving. They were imbued with the idea that any man could become a sailor if he wanted to or was hammered and pounded and abused into it, and, oddly enough, their theories were usually borne out to large extent and within a surprisingly short time the former landlubbers from parks, gutters, mills and farms were able to run aloft, to man yards and footropes, to tail onto halliards, braces and sheets; to reef the flapping beating sails and even to maintain a lookout from the topgallant crosstrees. Of course, many of them were utterly hopeless and were physically unable to go far up the rigging, while others never could learn the ropes, sails and rigging or could tell a halliard from a main-brace, no matter how hard the mates tried to beat such knowledge into their thick skulls. Usually, after a time, the mates decided that further efforts were merely a waste of energy and if the stupid chaps had not been seriously injured or killed in the process, they were detailed to deck duties and work which did not necessitate going aloft.

"But whether they showed proficiency in learning the rigging or not, there was one thing which they all could learn, and that was how to pull a boat. In comparison with going aloft the boat training was child's play and good fun, and every day, when the sea was smooth and the winds light, the boats were lowered away and the men were trained in handling them. At first their efforts were unspeakably awkward and comical, for the long ash oars were heavy and clumsy and the men had never touched or seen such things in all their lives; but they seemed to take to the work and very soon became adepts. They could pull in unison, could obey orders instantly and knew their duties, and a keen rivalry always sprang up between the various crews and they enjoyed nothing better than racing one another. At such times, they fairly lifted the big boats through the sea and put their very hearts and souls into the work. So too, they learned to handle their craft as silently as shadows when approaching a whale and occasionally one of the men would take enough interest and exhibit enough proficiency to be promoted to the rank of boat-steerer; but the majority remained mere 'hands' throughout the long cruises, and when at last they reached the home port, found that after being at sea for years, they had nothing coming from their 'lays,' as advances, supplies from the slop-chest and other items,—all charged at many times their value,—had more than exhausted their share of the catch. Seldom indeed did the men go to sea on a whaler more than once and they were glad enough to accept the tickets from the port to their home towns, content to step once more on dry land and betake themselves to their wonted haunts. It was very largely due to this fact that the whaling captains, mates and shipping agents could obtain crews and were able to treat the men as they did.

"The men were not 'seamen' and had no recourse to the sailors' aid societies; they were ignorant of the law and had no redress in that direction, and for that matter were often fugitives from justice or of a class whose sole idea of the law is to keep as far from it as possible, and as they had no intention of ever repeating their experience they let the whole matter drop. Even when they had opportunities to desert the ship in a foreign port they rarely did so, for they were penniless and seldom had a trade or occupation by which they could earn a living; they knew nothing of foreign ways or tongues; they were not real sailors and therefore could not find berths on other ships, and even if they knew enough to apply to the American consul as distressed seamen they were too fearful of the results when they reached home to take the chance.

"And while they were woefully beaten and abused, yet too much sympathy should not be wasted upon them. You must remember that they were largely of the roughest and toughest class, and to them, hard knocks, rotten food, filthy labor, foul air, and fouler quarters were merely incidents. To men who had always been accustomed to the endless toil of farm life the work aboard a whaler was simple and easy. To the man who went to sea to escape the life of a convict or the death of a felon anything was welcome. To the drunkard who is waked night after night by a policeman's club, a rope's-end would seem like a love-pat and to gutter snipes who depended upon garbage pails for their living the stinking, worm-eaten ship's fare would be a luxury. Most of them, no doubt, deserved all they got at the hands of the mates and their rough treatment resulted in making *men* of them, brave and efficient, hard working and strong as long as they were aboard ship, and the only pity is that their enforced reformation was not more enduring.

"Some ships were, of course, worse than others, for many mates and captains were humane, decent and really good-hearted men and treated their crews with no little kindness and consideration; but as a rule, the captains, and more particularly the mates, were brutal, drinking men without a spark of humanity or sentiment in their make-up and by years of whaling had become utterly calloused and indescribably cruel. While ashore they were obliged to keep themselves under control, but once at sea, and beyond the pale of the law, they became fiends in human form.

"The great wonder is that they were not worse than they were, for once the ships set sail from the western islands,—where they usually put in for fresh vegetables, fruits, water and native Portuguese whalers—they seldom touched ports for months, or even years, at a time. The further they cruised from frequented ports, the more chances they had of finding whales, and as long as they were on the high seas the skipper was supreme and utterly beyond all restraint of law or civilization.

"Voyages of from four to six years' duration were not unusual, and the constant monotony, the many vexations, the confinement and the surroundings developed all that was worst and most brutal in men's characters. Bad as was the lot of the crew on the best of whaling ships, one can scarcely imagine what it was when a captain and his mates were of the hard-fisted, hard-drinking, calloused type and had no other way of amusing themselves than to invent new tortures and abuses for their men. So awful were some of the cruelties practised, that stories of the acts reached authorities at home or abroad and occasionally the officers were arrested, tried and even convicted. But such cases were extremely rare, for the word of a common seaman had no weight and those who testified against their officers were sure of worse treatment later, while money from the ships' owners was always spent freely to secure the acquittal of mates or skippers. Many of the most awful deeds of such men will never be known, but in logbooks and journals, in the court records, the consular reports and other authentic sources, you may find tales of tortures and cruelties inflicted on the helpless men that seem incredible.

"One captain was in the habit of passing his leisure hours by ordering the men into the rigging and then shooting at them with his revolver. Another ordered one of his men stripped and scrubbed with lye and scouring-brick daily, and while the victim was driven insane by this treatment the captain escaped punishment and still lives, or did until recently, in New Bedford. It was a very common occurrence for the men to be strung up by their thumbs for hours at a time, and outright murder was frequently committed, sometimes in a fit of rage, at other times deliberately, and at other times to cover up injuries or mutilations which had been produced by torture. And strange as it may seem, these things were not all of the past. Scarcely a season goes by without some complaint of unbearable cruelties or murder being made, and only five years ago the mate of one schooner from this very port of New Bedford charged the skipper with gagging him with a belaying pin forced in his mouth and lashed by a rope around his head, in which condition he had been confined for a long period.

"No doubt many of these most inhuman captains were actually maniacs or were temporarily insane, for there are many instances on record of the whaling captains going mad on the subject of religion, or other matters. Oftentimes, these men, who were sanctimonious ashore and who became unbalanced through the loneliness of their lives and the ever present menace of death, endangered their ships and the lives of all on board, and as a rule they generally ended by committing suicide.

"But all this is very unpleasant and is the worst side of whaling and we can now turn to the brighter and more romantic events in the whalemen's lives where unparalleled bravery took the place of brutality; where skill and hardihood replaced knocks and blows, and where thrills and excitement, adventure and the constant peril of instant death were the lot of the men."

CHAPTER V

"AS I have already said, the whalemen's life was one of incessant drudgery, continual training and endless work from the time they gained the open sea until they reached the 'grounds,' or those portions of the ocean where whales were likely to be seen. Then everything but the hunt for their prey was given up and all attention was devoted to the business of the chase.

"From their lofty perches on the topgallant crosstrees, the lookouts sweep the sea with keen eyes, ever on the alert to catch the little blurr of vapor which denotes the presence of a spouting whale and to shout the glad cry of 'She blows!' to the officers and crew on deck. And, instantly at the words, the entire ship springs into life and activity. Men drop tasks or amusements and dash to their boats; hurriedly but with perfect precision the crafts are lowered away. The mainyard is swung and the ship hove-to, and in far less time than it takes to tell of it, the boats are off, dancing over the waves,—fairly steaming through the sea; as pulled by the long, ash oars and the brawny muscles of the men they tear away from the ship towards the giant creatures swimming lazily ahead.

"Presently, however, as the boats draw near the whales, the men row more slowly and every sound is hushed, for the whales have keen ears and can detect any unusual sound at a long distance. As silently and stealthily as ghosts the boats creep forward,—from the rear if the quarry is a sperm whale and from ahead if it is a right whale or bowhead,—and frequently the men draw in their oars and take to the paddles in order that no possible creak or rattle of a rowlock or splash of oars may frighten their prey or 'gally' it as the whalemen say.

"When near the monster the boat-steerer drops his oar, carefully lifts the heavy iron from its place, unsheathes the keen point, and standing erect in the bow, with every muscle taut, every nerve tense and every sense on the alert, makes ready to dart his weapon into the side of the unsuspecting creature as soon as he is within reach.

"Perhaps the whale may remain upon the surface and thus present an easy mark, or again, he may suddenly 'sound' or dive. In this case the rowers instantly cease their efforts and the boats remain motionless, waiting for the whale to come to the surface, and so familiar with the habits of the creatures are the veteran whalemen that they can tell by the way the whale sounds just where he will emerge or 'breach' to blow.

"Very often, too, the whale becomes 'gallied' or frightened and dashes off at terrific speed, and then commences a long, back-breaking, heart-rending chase with the boats striving their utmost to come within striking distance and the whale doing his best to evade the men. Often such a chase leads the men for miles away from their ship and continues for many hours, but as long as there is the least chance of getting 'fast' the boats pursue, doggedly and ceaselessly, until they either capture the whale or find themselves so far from their vessel that there is danger of becoming lost. Whether the whale lies quietly and allows the boats to close in, whether he sounds and the men rest on their oars until he breaches, or whether he leads them a long and weary chase, eventually the boat is brought within a score of feet of the gigantic black mass of flesh, bone and blubber which looks like nothing so much as the bottom of a capsized ship. But within that mountain of flesh lurks titanic strength, immeasurable power, terrific fury and a capability of wreaking death and destruction. Nearer and nearer creep the boats, until at last, when within a few paces, the mate shouts 'Give it to him!' and instantly at the cry the heavy iron is hurled with all the harpoonier's strength and the keen steel is buried deep in the body of the whale.

"Scarcely has the iron left his hand ere the boat-steerer leaps aft and seizes the huge steering oar, while the mate springs forward and takes his place at the bow, ready to kill the whale when opportunity offers. And then begins the most thrilling, most dangerous, and most exciting battle between man and beast which the world knows,—a fight to the death between the most powerful, the largest and the most dangerous of creatures and six men in a tiny boat.

THE BOYS' BOOK OF WHALERS

"Frightened and furious at the smart of the iron in his side, the whale dashes away with the line fastened to the harpoon roaring through the bow-chock and whirling from its tub like an uncoiling serpent. Possibly the wounded whale may tear onwards on a straight course for miles; again he may turn and twist and cut circles or 'mill,' or he may sulk or sound in his vain efforts to free himself from the stinging iron in his flesh. But no matter which course he follows every second is filled with deadly peril for the men, and the utmost skill and judgment and lightning-like activity must be constantly brought into play to save lives and boat. At any instant the whale may suddenly change his tactics and 'mill,' in which case the boat is liable to be capsized, despite the almost superhuman skill of the boat-steerer. If he dashes straight away, the boat may be carried out of sight of the ship and lost. If he sounds too fast or too deeply the line may be exhausted and the boat dragged under the sea unless instantly cut. And in addition to these, there are a thousand minor dangers to guard against. The whirring line must be kept free from kinks and must be kept from burning by water thrown upon it. If the line tangles or a coil kinks it may mean death or terrible injuries. Many a whaleman's leg has been torn off by the line leaping about it; many a whaleman has met an awful death by being dragged bodily beneath the sea by the whizzing line, and yet the rope must be kept taut by pulling in and coiling the slack at every opportunity, for only in this way can the boat be gradually worked closer and closer to the whale in order that the mate may give him his death blow. But the men give no heed to the dangers, no thought to the menace or the risk of life and limb; their one idea is to make a kill and the whaleman's motto is, 'A dead whale or a stove boat.'

"Every gesture, every word is obeyed instantly, for all realize that upon this depends their lives, as well as the capture of the whale, while the boat-steerer must use all the strength of his knotted muscles, every ounce of his weight, every atom of the skill which is his to swing and steer the rushing boat, to guide it safely on its mad career as it is towed by the wounded giant of the seas to which it is fast.

"Frequently two or more boats get fast to one

whale, but even so, the danger is no whit less and more often the battle is carried on by one boat's crew.

"Gradually the whale is tired; slower and slower become his mad dashes, shorter and shorter his soundings, and as the slack of line is hauled in the distance between boat and whale becomes less and less and with each foot and inch that the distance is decreased the perils of the men are increased a hundredfold. If the catch is a sperm whale there is the terrible, armed, lower jaw to be avoided, as well as the danger of a crushing blow from the immense tail, while, if the catch is a right whale a single sweep of the stupendous flukes may smash the boat to splinters and wound or kill its occupants. Moreover, there is not a chance of avoiding flukes or jaws. The men cannot dodge or retreat, for their craft is fast to the whale by the line and they must draw themselves into the very centre of the danger zone. Only the skill of the mate and his long, keen lance stand between them and instant death or worse, for the greatest danger, the utmost peril of the chase, lie in making the kill. Stung by a harpoon, the whale is frightened, and anxious only to rid himself of the iron and his tormentors, and seldom indeed will he turn to attack the boat. Moreover, in order to throw the iron it is not necessary to approach closer to the monster than fifteen feet. But when, tired and furious at his inability to escape, the whale at last realizes that the boat and its occupants are the cause of his troubles, he seeks only to destroy them and waits only for them to come within reach of his trip-hammer flukes or his crashing, death-dealing, many-toothed jaw. Of course if the whale is to be killed by a bomb-lance there is not so much danger, for the explosive charge may be fired into the whale from a fairly safe distance; but when killing with the old-time hand-lance the boat must be brought right alongside the monster in order that the mate may *shove* the lance into the whale's vitals by main strength, for, unlike the harpoon, the lance is *pushed* into the whale's body and is not thrown.

"Try to imagine what it means to be in a tiny boat beside a wounded giant whale, to be so close to a mountain of concentrated strength and fury that the lance point may be placed *against* his side, to know that without an instant's warning the creature may turn and crush boat and crew in his awful jaws or may throw it a score of feet in air, broken, crushed and splintered, with a stroke of the gigantic tail. Try to imagine this and you will begin to realize the supreme courage, the wonderful self-reliance, the sublime faith in their mate and the marvelously steady nerves which the whalemen possess.

"And the dangers are not ended by any means when at last the boat is alongside the whale, and with a grunt by the mate, the keen lance is driven into the creature. On the contrary, the greatest peril of all is that which follows, for rarely does a whale die instantly or quietly but instead struggles and fights in his death-throes or 'flurry' and many a whaleman's life has been lost, many a boat smashed to matchwood by the dying efforts of a lanced whale.

"Lifting his stupendous head far above the sea and bringing it crashing down with the force of falling mountain; snapping, thrusting, biting to right and left with his sharp-toothed, enormous jaw; spouting blood until the sea is crimson; swinging his ponderous flukes and lashing the waves into froth and foam, a sperm whale in his flurry fights to his last gasp and will destroy everything within reach. And close in to this maniacal, pain-crazed, writhing giant the whaleboat is tossed about, thrown hither and thither on the blood-stained waves churned up by his thrashing flukes, and every instant is menaced by the crashing tail, the descending head and the terrible jaw. Striving like madmen to avoid destruction, handling their craft with superhuman skill, escaping as by a miracle a score of times in as many seconds, the whalemen remain within the maelstrom of death until at last the cry of 'fin up' roars forth and the whale rolls upon his side,—dead.

"If no other whales are in sight, chains are passed about his tail and he is towed to the ship as I have already described; but if, on the other hand, more whales were in the vicinity a small flag on an iron staff, and known as a 'waif,' is planted in the whale's body and the weary men start off to attack the next victim; perchance to make a kill without casualties, perhaps to have their boat stove in, and often to have bones broken or to meet with death.

THE BOYS' BOOK OF WHALERS

"Although the whales were often taken close to the ships, yet the majority were finally killed miles away, and with the vessels hove-to and with only a few men to handle them it was essential that they should have a well understood set of signals to use in case of necessity. If a storm was brewing or darkness fell it was necessary to recall the boats. If other whales were sighted it was important that the boats should be notified. If one of the boats was stove the other boats must be sent to its assistance. These and a thousand other incidents might arise which the boats' crews must know, and while they could see their ship and watch her for signals yet they might not be able to see other boats or whales and depended upon their ship's signals to locate them. Moreover, from the ship's mastheads, the boats and any whales in the neighborhood could be watched even when miles away, and when the hulls of the vessels were below the horizon from the boats. Very often, the distance was so great that signal flags could not be distinguished, and, as a result, the whalemen adopted signals given either with sails alone or by means of sails combined with yards and colors with the addition of a 'masthead-waif' which was a hoop covered with canvas and placed at the end of an eight-foot staff. As several ships were frequently in sight at the same time each had its own set or code of signals to avoid confusion; but all were more or less similar. For example, a flag at the foremast might mean whales in sight; colors at half mast would signify that whales were between the ship and the boats; if the jib were up it might mean that whales were on the starboard bow; the main topgallant sail on the cap would tell the boats that whales were on the lee bow; colors, or the waif, at fore and main masts sent news of a stove boat, while a signal at the mizzen would recall all boats.

"Thus, as long as the boats could see their ship's spars, they were in touch with all that was going on and knew that they were under the watchful eyes of their skipper and that perfect confidence could be placed upon him and his signals.

"Many times, however, the night came on or a storm arose long before the boats could gain their vessel's side, or at other times they were

THE BOYS' BOOK OF WHALERS

towed so far that not even the lofty trucks of their ship were visible and on every side stretched the restless, tossing waves. In either case, the men were in grave danger and many a boat has thus been lost never to be heard from again, while others, after voyages of thousands of miles over the trackless ocean, have been picked up by another ship or have safely reached some distant shore. But that is a story which we must put over to another day."

CHAPTER VI

WHEN the boys went to the museum on the following day, they found their friend studying an old, weather-stained book, while before him on the table were piles of big volumes; some bound in worn, rusty leather; others in discolored parchment; a few in heavy, mildewed canvas, and all showing signs of hard usage, great age and frequent handling.

"Why, those are logbooks!" exclaimed Harry, as he glanced at the cover of the nearest.

"Yes, whalemen's logs," replied the curator. "So far I've told you the most important facts about whales, whale ships and whalemen. About their lives and dangers; how they capture, cut-in and boil down the whales and what the whaling industry meant to New England. Now I'm going to introduce you two boys to the real life of the whalemen through the medium of their own words as written in these old logs. Of course, much of their contents are uninteresting and

THE BOYS' BOOK OF WHALERS

consist only of the records of work done, money expended, courses run, the weather encountered and similar matters; but, tucked in amid this mass of humdrum data, are stories as fascinating and thrilling, as full of adventure and bloodshed, as humorous and as pathetic as any books of fiction ever written. Moreover, by reading them, one may get a very good insight into the characters of the men, their hopes, fears and thoughts. From them, too, one may learn much of real value and interest such as the size and number of whales taken, the quantity of oil secured, descriptions of strange, out-of-the-way places and the habits of little-known people. Unlike the merchantmen, the whalers entered everything in their logs, whether it had anything to do with the ship, the voyage or their cargoes, for the whaleman's log was really a journal and everything which transpired ashore or aboard was set down in quaint phrases and sentences and curiously misspelled words. Even family matters, such as wedding anniversaries, birthdays, etc., were entered, as were such trivial matters as the killing of a fowl for dinner or the fact that a ship's cat had kittens. Moreover, the whaling captains made use of their logs for figuring up sums in arithmetic, in keeping memorandums of business transactions and in writing letters, and many of the margins of their pages are as interesting as the real entries. In addition, many were illustrated with pen and ink, pencil or colored drawings, for time hung as heavily on the officers' hands as on the men's and they wrote their logs as they would have written letters or stories.

"Even those which were not illustrated are full of quaint pictures such as these. Here you see a black silhouette showing a sperm whale, while below it is a whale's tail, also in solid black, which indicates that a whale sounded, and beside this is a half whale horizontally placed which shows that a whale 'drew' or escaped. These were symbols printed from blocks carved by the whalemen and which were very useful, for not only was it easier to use this picture writing than to laboriously spell out and write words but by means of these symbols printed on the margins of the pages the reader could tell at a glance how many whales had escaped, how many were taken, just how they acted and the number

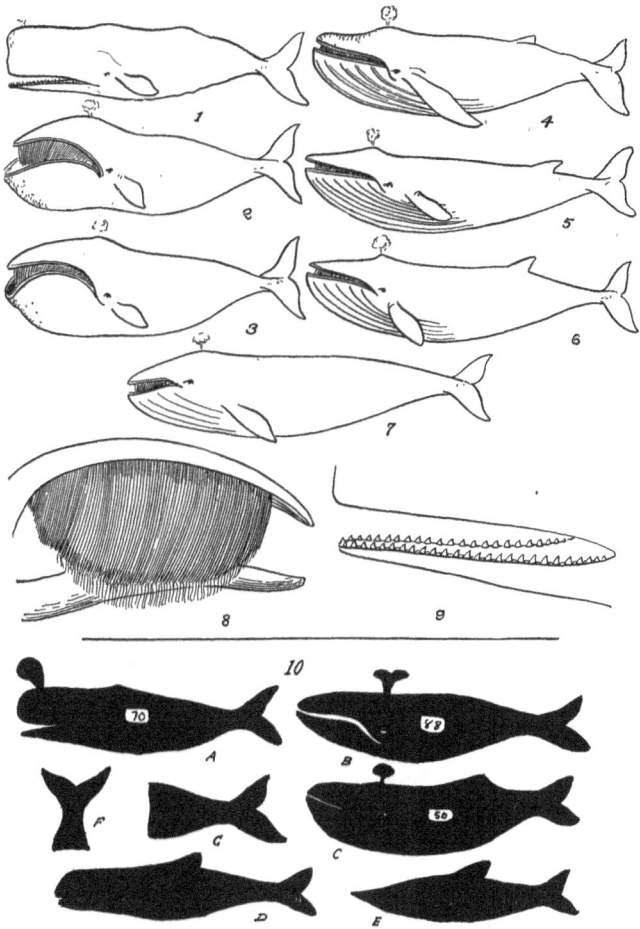

EXPLANATION—KINDS OF WHALES, SYMBOLS, ETC.

Sperm Whale
Bowhead Whale
Right Whale
Humpback Whale
Sulphur Bottom Whale
Fin Back Whale
California Gray Whale
Jaws of Right Whale showing whalebone or baleen
Jaws of Sperm Whale showing teeth
Symbols used by whalemen in their log books

A Sperm whale (70 bbls.) taken
B Right whale or Bowhead (88 bbls.)
C Humpback whale (50 bbls.)
D Grampus
E Porpoise
F Whale sounded
G Iron drew or whale lost

of barrels obtained from each, for the quantity of oil taken from each whale was noted on a small white spot left upon the whale's body for that purpose. Most of these pictures were printed in plain black ink, but in one book here the captain used blue ink and added to the realism by painting in plumes of red spray to indicate that the whales 'spouted blood' or were killed.

"Many whalers cruised for both right and sperm whales and had stamps to indicate each kind, while some of the logs are so filled with prints of porpoises, walruses, seals, sea elephants, grampuses, narwhals, etc., that they look like marine menageries or children's animal books. Nowadays rubber stamps of conventional design are used in place of the old-fashioned crudely carved wooden ones and are not half as interesting.

"I have already said that the logs were practically journals, but the officers, and even members of the crews, often kept their private diaries and journals and in these we may often find entries which are even more interesting than those in the logbooks. Unfortunately, the whalemen's families and friends often considered their old books of no value and many of the best and most interesting were lost or destroyed. I have tried to select some of the most interesting or humorous from those in the museum and I'll read the more striking or peculiar entries to you.

"Some of the logs were really pathetic and filled with sadness from end to end; others were hopeful and jolly; others told of long cruises with only empty casks and bitter disappointments as a result, while a few were penned by men evidently on the verge of madness. Here, for example, is the log of the New Bedford ship *Morea* which set sail on the 13th of October, 1853, and returned May 1st, 1856. Oddly enough, several other ships, which at various times set sail on the thirteenth of the month, met with tragedies of the sea and yet the whalemen never looked with superstition upon thirteen as did the merchantmen. The first entries in the *Morea's* log which were made by the skipper are of no particular interest, so we will skip the pages until we come to the date of June 3rd, 1854, where we find the entries signed by the chief mate, Beriah C. Manchester. His first entry is as follows:

"'Remarks on board the Ship *Morea*, Sat., June 3rd, 1854.

"'Strong winds from WNM and some fog. The first part ship head SE. Saw five ships. This afternoon Captain Peabody retired for a while and on being Called and at the tea table he made some very unusual remarks from him to make, askin the officers if they thought a man would be punished in the other world for making away with himself if he had nothing to hope for or could see no prospect of happiness before him. At night he went to bed as usual and was up during the night givin directions how to stear. At breakfast he seemed rather melancolly, eat little and after breakfast come on deck but soon went below again. At 10 A. M. he sent the Steward after mee to come below. I went into the cabbin. Hee told mee hee had sent for mee to tell mee that hee was goin to meet his God and gave mee his reasons for doing so and some little directions about his things. After conversing with him for some twenty minutes or more I went on deck and communicated that hee had told mee to the other officers.

"'Soon after wee three—the second and third mates and myself—went down and inquired if he had tacon anything to caus him to bee as hee was. At first hee said no only a spoonful of Brandy but soon after on being asked again hee said hee would not go with a lie for hee had tacon landanum; but as wee thought hee had not tacon enough to caus death wee let him bee. Hee now inquired how the weather was. At marideon hee got up, called for a light lit a cigar and went to bed again. So this affair stood at noon. Midale and last of this day fresh SW winds and cloudy weather. One man sick.

" 'Remarks Sunday June 4th, 1854.
" 'Strong South winds and some rain etc. At 2 P. M. Capt. Peabody got up and wanted an observation tacon but hee was in sutch a state hee was not able to note the time. Hee remained up till 6.30 p. m. while up gave his opinion on the prospect of whales at certain places then went to bed again. At 9 P. M. hee gave orders to lay the head yards back. At 2.30 a. m. hee gave orders to stear north as soon as it was light enough to man the mast head. At breakfast hee said hee could not eat anything Hee seemed in his right mind through the forenoon. At dinner time I asked him if hee could eat some dinner. Hee said his thoughts of food made him sick to his stomak but said the Steward was going to make some soup, Etc.

"'Monday June 5th, 1854. About 2 P. M. saw two whales. Lowered three boats. At 3 returned on board without getting fast. While the boats was off Capt. Peabody gave orders to make more sail and keep the ship near the boats and after wee got aboard hee asked mee how many whales I saw. At tea time he was in bed and did not get up. At 6.30 p. m. saw two whales the weather was too thick to lower. While looking at the whales their being no one in the cabin but the captain, wee heard the report of a gun and a musket ball come through the deck. We immediately went below and found Capt. Peabody lying on deck in his room with his face blown off from his chin to his eyes both upper and lower jaws entirely off. Hee breathed a few minutes and was gone. Middle part more moderate. At 1.30 a. m. saw ice, then at rest. At 8.30 a. m. committed the remains of Captain Peabody to the deep and A solemn right it was indeed. Thus ends these 24 hours.'

"That," continued the curator, "is an excellent illustration of the way that the whaleman had of entering the most tragic events in the plainest and most cursory manner along with the state of weather, the whales taken and similar matters. Now let us turn from such a doleful log to cheery logs of good luck and pleasant voyages. This, from the log of the Nantucket ship *Ohio* is a good example.

" 'Remarks on board the ship *Ohio* of Nantucket. Chas. W. Coffin, Master. Cruising off Japan. Friday July 17th, 1834.
" 'First part light breezes at S. W. Lie up N. E. under full sail employed repairing foretopmast and staysail finished bent it wet the hold. At sunset shortened sail. Middle part much the same. At daylight commenced stowing down at 9 A. M. saw a shoal of spern whales. Put off at 11 A. M. struck, the boats among whales. N. Lat 31.'

"Here is another entry from the ship *Montreal:*

" 'In the Kamtskatkal Sea. F. L. Fish, Master. Thursday July the 15th, 1851.
" 'These 24 hours commenced with a light air and cloudy from the south and westward the boats off chasing whales At 3 P. M. struck 2 whales and turned them up 7 miles from the ship in a calm at 11 took them alongside with fresh breeze from the S at 1 A. M. all hands sent below at 7 called all hands and commenced cutting in. Latter part puffy with a light air and a

berg heavy swell from S. all hands employed cutting At 12 M had one whale in and hooked on to the other. So ends. Lat 60° 53' North.'

"What a contrast to these terse entries, telling of good catches, is this log of the *Minnesota* written by Captain Clothier Pierce, a strange character apparently, for he always spoke of his ship as 'The Most Unfortunate Vessel in the Whaling Business' and invariably cried whenever he made an entry in his log. In fact, his entire time seems to have been occupied in dismal forebodings and tearful lamentations. He was such a sad and melancholy man that one really pities him, but his forebodings were wasted and ere the end of his doleful voyage he made a good catch. It would be tiresome to read all his entries but here are a few samples:

"'Remarks on board the Most Unfortunate Vessel in the Whaling Business July 1, 1868. No signs of life here, nothing for us. June has passed and we get now where. No chance for us this season I fear. Three seasons in the North Atlantic too get one whale in this unfortunate vessel.'

* * * * * * *

"'July 4th. Wind E. S. E. Will the wind never change? This is the Fourth of July a day of rejoicing with People at Home. But a sad day for us. No whales in The Ocean that we can Find. A Head Wind. No chance to do anything or to even get one whale.

"'The Lord's Hand appears to be against the poor old Minnesota and all concerned in her. Will the Lord in His infinite Mercy ever suffer us to get one Whale? Employed sheathing the deck. Many are rejoicing to-day but our hearts are filled with sadness that this Poor Vessel cannot get a whale.'

* * * * * * *

"'July 12th. Nothing to be seen but sails. I fear the ocean contains no treasures for this unfortunate vessel. Nothing like sperm whales here. Picked up a barrel of petroleum oil. So the time passes and we get Nothing.'

* * * * * * *

"'July 13th. No whale this season for the poor Old Minnesota. The Lord will not suffer us to get one I am so wicked. Fate has ordained that we get nothing this season. May the Lord in His Mercy pour out a blessing for this unfortunate vessel is my earnest prayer although I feel I am unworthy. May that Being that presides over the destinies of men guide and direct me in all things I desire. Some fog. Bad weather for seeing. A perfect desert. The Pierce family are unfortunate. Looks desolate. Our ruin is inevitable.'

"Here, for variety, is the log of a ship whose steward was a poet and not only entered his verses in the ship's log which he kept but wrote very credible prose also. The ship was the schooner *Emmeline* of Mystic, Connecticut, on a cruise to the Croisette Islands for sea-elephant oil, and the steward's name was Washington Foster,—the date 1843. On Christmas day the schooner was at anchor at the Croisettes and to celebrate the occasion, Foster wrote the following parody on 'The Old Oaken Bucket':

"'How dear to this heart are the scenes of past days.
When fond recollection recalls them to mind.
The schooner so taut and so trim like a miss in her stays.
And all her light rigging which swayed to the wind.
The old fashioned galley, the try-works close by it.
The old blubber boat with six oars to pull it.
The bunk of my messmate, the wooden chest nigh it,

The old Monkey Jacket, the often patched jacket. The greasy old jacket which hung up beside it.'

"Then follows a long dissertation on the weather, the difficulties in reaching the shore and then the following:

"'We had almost forgotten that to-day is Christmas day, the season of festivity and rejoicing at home and we can almost fancy we hear the halls resounding with the enlivening notes of the violin and the merry step of the fascinating dance, the tables groaning under the weight of poultry pies and all the delicacies of the season, and—but stop, the bark of that infernal sea-elephant had destroyed the illusion and recalled our wandering senses back to our anchorage in the cold, stormy, cheerless and desolate Croisettes. But no matter, 'tis true we cannot at present revel amid the strong exhilirating mixtures and quaff the luxurious wines of the season, being at present all hands of us "teetotallers" but we can look forward to St. Helena and a full ship and in sweet anticipation lay back to a bottle of Cunningham's best and that is almost as good as though we had it. Moreover, we can,—listen to me now ye epicures who ransack ocean, earth and air to satisfy your pampered and vitiated appetites,—we live, nay we feast, here in this remote and dismal corner of the globe, on luxuries the savoury flavor of which you can form no conception. The richest and most delicious morsels of food that ever found their way into human stomach, such as sea-elephants' tongues, flippers, hearts, livers and tripe etc so that we are not so bad off during the holidays, but that we might be much worse.'

"Evidently a man of some education and talent and possessed with an optimistic heart and good spirits was this steward of the *Emmeline*. It seems as though he should have found a better fate than being steward of a grease-soaked whaler, and we must hope that he arrived safely at his Connecticut home and spent the next Christmas among the scenes and festivities he loved so well. Among the logs, too, we will sometimes find stories of mutinies, but such are very rare, for as a rule the mutineers destroyed ship and logs if they were successful. Sometimes, however, the mutiny was nipped in the bud or the officers quelled it, as was the case of that on the ship *Barclay*, and fortunately, the *Barclay's* log is preserved. Although trouble began to brew soon after the ship sailed, yet as nothing serious occurred for some time we may as well skip the first few entries and begin with the date of Monday, October 6th, 1834:

" 'Commenseed with fine weather and light Winds from the South. We with all sails set. One Brig in sight at 2 o'clock. Lowered our boats to exercise the crew which was very necesury. At supper While in the act of shareing the vittals forward, one of the Crew began to fight with some of the Green hands, it being the third time. We put him in Rigging Not intending to flay him, but his sarsy tung caused him a few stripes with fore parts if a small head line affter which he acknowledge he was to blame. We then let him go forward where he made nomber threats. This promising youth's name is Bradford Trafford. Mid part airs from the South The Blacksmuths very sausy, he being the worse for Rum. Latt. part calmer, lowered the boats and chaseed Grampass for whales.

" 'Oct. 8th. Nothing to be seen but the wide Ocean. Our old Rigging parts very often, it is not otherwise to be expected. So ends this long and Dismal day in hopes of a fare one.'

"But despite hopes, the 'fare' weather did not arrive and for days the ship was buffeted by

THE BOYS' BOOK OF WHALERS

'Heavy Gails' as she worked her way around Cape Horn and into the Pacific despite her rotten rigging. Indeed, so rough was the weather that entries were not made in the log for a long time, the next one of note being dated Friday, April 29th, and reads as follows:

"'At 8 o'clock the Captain sent the steward forward to Call the Men Aft or one of them, to see their Meat Weighed; but their reply was that they would not come. This was told the Captain. He immediately Called to them to come aft and repeated it three times and then went after them and took a Broom at one of the Blacks. They all refused to go aft but one said one of their complaint was that one pound and one quarter of meat was not enough and were very insolent and made their threats. They Now went Forward not wishing to see their weight of meat the said Black was insolent to the Captain when Coming Forward but was called to Go Aft again, his reply was that he would not and fled for the foreCastle. While getting him up one of the Men Henry Ketchum came at the Gangway and interfered and Challenged the Captain and struck him. At this time the Captain took hold of him and dropped his wepon. The Fellow took it up and maid attempt to strike the Captain. From this he was told to go Aft but refused and went Down the Fore Castle. Took a sheath knife and said he would kil the first man that went down but afterwards delivered himself to be put in Irons where now remains in the Run. Thus ends in Peace.'

"And now let me read you some entries from what is most probably the strangest and most humorous log in existence, the log, or rather the journal, of the bark *Alexander*, which set sail in 1835 and which was kept by the cooper, Ephraim Billings, the captain and mates being so drunk throughout the voyage that they could not keep either log nor journal. We can imagine, after looking over his entries in the journal, that the poor cooper had a hard time of it, and while we must laugh as we read over his quaint entries and remarks, yet to Billings it was all a most serious and important matter. Funnily enough, too, the cooper never wrote in the first person, but always mentioned himself as if speaking of some one else, and we find such entries as, 'This day is the birthday of Ephraim Billings, cooper of the bark *Alexander*,' or 'The cooper remained on board, the others being ashore drunk.'

THE BOYS' BOOK OF WHALERS

"During the first part of the cruise the cooper tried his best to enter the daily events faithfully, but as he soon found that they were most monotonous and consisted mainly of such items as: 'The skipper came aboard drunk,' 'The mate was very drunk,' 'All hands but the cooper were drunk,' he soon became discouraged or careless and only mentioned the unusual or remarkable things which happened, such as, 'The mate was only a little drunk,' 'Skipper not very drunk,' or, once in a great while, the startling information that 'The captain was not drunk to-day.' Only on one day throughout the entire voyage did he have anything to the officers' credit to enter in his journal and that was when the captain administered a deserved thrashing to a mutinous and insolent boy, and Ephraim remarked that 'This is the best deed the captain has yet done on this terrible voyage, pray God he may repeat the work often.'

"Evidently Billings remained sober throughout the voyage, although he must have been the only member of the ship's company who was, for he never failed to make some entry each day and never forgot to note the anniversary of his birth, of the death of his wife or of his wedding, and always underscored such things with heavy, black lines. He was apparently the only one who ever gave any thought to the welfare of the bark, and, reading between the lines of his journal, we can see that the poor man was horribly homesick and lonely. With such officers and crew there is little wonder that no whales were secured, for captain, mates and men alike spent all their time in drinking and debauchery. At last, however, the cooper's troubles came to an end, for in a South American port the drunken skipper had him placed under arrest on the charge of mutiny. And this was, perhaps, the most humorous thing which occurred on the whole trip and the culmination of all the other acts performed by the befuddled skipper, for the 'mutiny' consisted of the cooper coming on deck in his stocking feet!

"Ephraim evidently found the cell in a South American prison far better and more comfortable than his berth aboard ship, and when the captain at last became sober enough to realize what he had done and begged the cooper to return to the bark, Billings flatly refused and in his journal, which he took to prison with him, he remarks that he did so, 'As God knows I know too much of what goes on and what I may expect.' Soon afterwards he was released and had a well-earned reward by being entertained by the officials until he was finally sent home in another ship, a wiser if not a sadder man, to settle down ashore for life, for, as his last entry, he wrote, 'Never to go a-whaling again, please God!'

"These are but a few examples of the whalemen's logs and journals, and one could read hundreds of them and always find something of interest, of tragedy or of amusement in their pages; but the most thrilling incidents were never recorded as the logs of the vessels where they took place were either destroyed or lost. There are few professions in the world so filled with danger, adventure and incredible incidents as the whaleman's, and yet they were all taken as part of the day's work by officers and men. It would take volumes to relate all of the disasters, mutinies and tragedies which took place, but I will tell you a few of the most noteworthy and famous to-morrow."

CHAPTER VII

"CAPTAIN NED told us a story of a whaler," said Bob as the boys met the curator the next day. "It was about a man named Jenkins who was carried under the water by a sperm whale and afterwards was thrown into his boat."

"Yes, and he insisted it was true," added Harry. "We didn't believe it at first, but Father said he had seen an account of it in a logbook."

"Yes, the log describing it is preserved," the curator assured him. "The story of Jenkins is absolute fact, incredible as it may seem; but there are many other stories of whaling which are fully as remarkable, while many of the accounts of mutinies, attacks by cannibals and shipwrecks are as exciting and thrilling as any tales of fiction."

"Ned told us another about a mutiny, too," put in Harry, "in which the men threw everything overboard so the captain had to give up the cruise."

"Yes," smiled the other, "that occurred on the *Pedro Varela*,—you can see her masts above the warehouse yonder if you look out of this window,—it was a unique sort of mutiny and more amusing than serious."

"Don't the whales ever attack the ships?" asked Bob. "I read a story once of a ship smashed by a whale."

"Yes, there are several records of whaling vessels being sunk by mad or frightened whales," replied the curator. "I'll tell you of some of those and also of ships that were wrecked by running onto sleeping whales, but suppose we group the stories together and take up those of each class in regular order.

"Of course," the curator continued, "the whalers had to face all the ever present dangers of the sea which confront ships and sailors of all kinds and, in addition, there were perils which beset the whalemen and which never menaced the merchant ships and merchant seamen. But notwithstanding this, and the fact that the whaleman's life was one of tremendous risk and that he constantly took his life in his hands, the loss of life and of ships was smaller in proportion than in any other profession of the sea.

"Collisions at sea, especially in foggy weather; sinking of ships by storms, being driven on reefs or rocks; ships being disabled and abandoned; fire; ships being lost by missing their course and running aground, are the commonest causes of loss of vessels and lives in the merchant service, and, oddly enough, very few of the whalers' losses were due to any of these. In fact, the dangers which are most feared by merchantmen never troubled the whalemen, and very few of their casualties were due to them.

"And this is the more remarkable when we consider that the whalers never kept to well-known routes or seas as did other ships; that they visited the least-known portions of the world; that in a single cruise they often spent more time at sea than would fall to the lot of merchant sailors in a lifetime, and that their ships were not uncommonly in such a state that no self-respecting merchantman would dream of going to sea in them.

THE BOYS' BOOK OF WHALERS

"Perhaps it was partly due to the fact that men who daily faced death in a hundred forms looked upon ordinary hazards of the sea with contempt; perhaps it was owing to the fact that the whale ships were heavily and strongly built and that seaworthiness was not sacrificed for speed or comfort, or maybe it was because the whalemen,—or at least the officers,—were such resourceful, splendid sailors. Whatever the reason, the fact remains that when we consider the great number of whale ships which were devoted to the business through more than two hundred years, the long voyages they took, the risks they ran and the uncharted seas they sailed, the total losses were marvelously small.

"Terrible indeed was the gale or storm which could dismast or injure the whale ships. They went unscathed through the most tempestuous seas; they weathered the hurricanes of the Antilles and the typhoons of the Orient; they fought the ice-laden, howling gales of Cape Horn and were battered by the bergs and floes of the Arctic. For years at a time they cruised amid the innumerable sharp-fanged reef of the Polynesians; they were pathfinders among the unknown islets and submerged rocks of the South Seas; they skirted the shores of every continent and sailed on every sea and seldom did they touch bottom. And even when a ship did go ashore, her giant oaken timbers and thick planking would stand a vast amount of buffeting without breaking up. Of course, out of the thousands of whale ships which first and last have sailed forth from New England ports, many never were heard from again; many a ship left her skeleton to mark her last resting-place on some desolate reef or beach thousands of miles from home; many foundered at sea and many were destroyed by fire; but the majority held their own for generation after generation of hardy skippers and still are strong, staunch and seaworthy to-day. Take, for example, the ship which first aroused your curiosity,—the bark *Betsey,*—she has just set forth on a three-years' cruise to the South Seas and yet the old ship is nearly one hundred years old,—she was built in Fairhaven, across the harbor, in 1840, and for more years than either of you boys have lived she has been laid up on a mud flat with grass and weeds growing from her seams, and yet, now, she sets forth to brave the stress and storms of the vast oceans for three long years on end.

"Scores of old whaling captains spent their lives at sea in the same ship and never had an accident and never lost a life. I know one old captain over eighty years of age who can boast that during all the years he has been to sea—and he started as a boy—his vessel never touched bottom, no man was ever lost or abandoned by his ship and that never had a single member of his crews been unfit for duty through accident or illness for more than a week at a time. Moreover, he can truthfully claim that in all those years he never lost but one spar, that he never came into port without a full cargo of oil and that never a day has passed at sea when he did not personally go aloft. And you must not imagine that his is an exceptional case. I could give you the names of at least fifty,—and there were hundreds who are dead and gone,—who could boast as much, or perhaps more, for the Yankee whaling skippers were born seamen, marvelous navigators, absolutely fearless, hard workers; men with iron nerve and muscles of steel, and men who never shirked duty. Through storm and calm, through balmy breeze or howling gale, when cruising on broiling tropic seas or working their way through the fog-shrouded ice-floes of the Polar regions, they piloted their ships a thousand times around the globe, following the whales across the seven seas and the five oceans, and ninety-nine times out of a hundred brought them safely back to port with all hands accounted for. In a general way, all the accidents that befell whale ships may be grouped in a few classes, although there were a few instances of unique disasters, while the losses among the boats and men were due to so many and such varied causes that each must be considered by itself.

"You spoke of ships being attacked by whales, so it may be just as well to take up stories of such disasters first. Perhaps the most notable record of a ship being rammed by a whale is that of the ship *Essex*, of Nantucket, and, moreover, this is the first known instance of the kind, although doubtless other ships had met a similar fate previously, but as all hands were lost no records were kept and the unfortunate vessels were merely posted among the missing. And, in addition, the story of the *Essex* is one of the most fearful tragedies of the sea of which there are authentic details.

"It was on the twelfth of August, 1819, that the *Essex* sailed from Nantucket under command of Captain George Pollard, Jr., bound for the Pacific, and no unusual event occurred on the long voyage southward and around Cape Horn. Reaching the Pacific, the *Essex* cruised about until November 29th, when a sperm whale was sighted and at the call of 'There she blows!' boats were lowered, the ship was hove-to and the men pulled lustily for the whale. The first boat alongside the creature was that in charge of the chief mate, but no sooner was he struck than, with a single sweep of his flukes, he stove in the frail boat and to save their lives the men cut the line. By stuffing their garments into the holes in the boat's planking and by constant bailing the crew managed to reach the *Essex* without mishap. In the meantime, the captain and the second mate had struck a whale and were fast, and the chief mate made sail on the ship and headed the vessel towards them.

"The mate was on the quarter-deck, and the

men were at work repairing their smashed boat when, within a score of rods from the ship, an eighty-five-foot whale suddenly breached from the water and, heading directly for the *Essex*, crashed into her with terrific speed.

"The monster struck the ship just forward of the foremast, and for a few minutes lay as if stunned by the force of the blow, and then, regaining its senses, he turned and swam off to leeward.

"The first blow had sprung a leak and the mate at once ordered the pumps manned and also set signals to recall the boats to the ship. Hardly had this been done when the whale again appeared, thrashing the sea into foam with his flukes and snapping his gigantic jaws, and after remaining motionless for an instant, as if to gather all his strength, he again rammed the ship, striking her with such irresistible force that he completely staved in the heavy planking close to the catheads.

"Seeing that it was useless to attempt to save the ship, the mate and the crew managed to get their injured boat into the water and scrambled into it. And not a moment too soon, for within two minutes after being struck by the maddened whale, the *Essex* went over on her beam-ends.

"In a few moments Captain Pollard arrived in his boat and ordered the men to cut away the ship's masts in the hopes that the vessel would right herself and float, which she did. Then holes were cut through the decks in order to reach a few of the stores in the upper part of the hold, and for three days the boats remained by the sinking ship while they built up the sides of their boats and repaired the one stove in by the first whale. At the close of the third day the heavy seas had widened the gaping hole made in the ship's side by the whale and the *Essex* began to go to pieces. As nothing more could be done, the three tiny boats turned about, and, leaving their sinking ship to its fate, headed for the nearest land—the coast of Peru, fully 3,000 miles distant.

"Think of it, boys! Three frail boats, one of which had been already strained and smashed, adrift in mid-Pacific with barely enough water and food to maintain life for a week,—for they had been unable to obtain more,—and with the nearest land 3,000 miles away! But the stout-hearted men never lost courage and toiled doggedly at their long oars. Broiled by the tropic sun, their lips and tongues swollen and parched with the salt spray; with barely a spoonful of water a day for each; faint and weak with hunger, they rowed day and night from the twenty-third until the twenty-eighth of November, when their bloodshot eyes were greeted with Ducie's Island, a barren, desolate speck in mid-ocean. Here there was no water, but a few shell-fish and sea-birds were found, and, forbidding as was the place, and while it meant certain death to remain, yet three of the men refused to leave, as they preferred to die upon the tiny bit of land rather than endure the awful agonies of hunger and thirst in the boats.

"Leaving Ducie's Island on the twenty-seventh of December, the boats resumed their almost hopeless voyage, and terrible as had been their sufferings before, yet they were nothing compared to the tortures the men endured on this awful row of 2,500 miles towards the Island of Juan Fernandez, off Peru.

"Day by day the men died, the first being the second mate, who succumbed on the tenth of

January, and two days after his death the boats became separated, two of them, those of the captain and second mate, remaining together until the twenty-ninth of January. By this time four other men had died and as fast as life left their bodies their comrades fell upon them, cut them to pieces and devoured the raw flesh like famished wolves. Then, when once more on the verge of starvation, the captain ordered that the men should draw lots to see who should be killed to keep the others alive. Twenty-four days later the ship *Dauphin,* of Nantucket, appeared upon the horizon, and bearing down upon the weather-beaten whaleboat, rescued Captain Pollard and Charles Ramsdale, the sole survivors of the boat's crew.

"In the meantime—on the seventeenth of February—the chief mate's boat had been sighted by the British brig *Indian,* and the three survivors it had contained had been saved, while the third boat never was heard from. The five survivors of this awful tragedy recovered, and in later years the *Essex's* captain found employment upon Fulton's famous steamboat, the *Hudson.*

"But the crews of other ships which have been

rammed by whales had far more fortunate experiences. For example, there was the *Ann Alexander,* a New Bedford ship under Captain John Deblois, which set sail from here on January 1st, 1858. Everything went well until the twentieth of August, when the chief mate struck a whale and made fast. No sooner did the creature feel the smart of the iron than he turned, rushed at the boat with open jaws and with a single crunch smashed it to matchwood. Seeing the predicament of his men, the captain abandoned the chase, and pulling with all speed to the assistance of the swimming men, dragged them into his boat and started for the ship.

"Meanwhile, those on the *Alexander* had also seen the accident, and, lowering the water-boat, headed for the captain who, with his overcrowded boat, was in constant danger. Dividing the crew between the two boats the fearless men again attacked the infuriated whale, only to have him turn again and stave in the second boat.

"With eighteen men crowded into the one remaining boat, the craft was loaded to the water's edge, and knowing it useless to attempt to capture the whale under such conditions, the overloaded boat was headed towards the ship, which was now between six and seven miles away. But scarcely had they started before the maddened whale appeared, and with wide-opened jaws rushed at the boat and every one thought that their last moment had come. Then, for some unexplained reason, the monster veered off when close at hand and tore past within a few feet of the boat.

"As soon as the men gained their ship the boat was sent back to pick up the oars, fittings and equipment of the stove boats, and while doing this, the whale again appeared and the men, still undaunted by their hairbreadth escapes, once more started for him. But when almost within striking distance the whale sounded, the chase was given up and the boat headed for the approaching vessel.

" Standing at the ship's bows, the captain was watching his boat, when, close to the vessel, the whale rose suddenly, and before a word could be uttered or an order given, he had struck the doomed ship, staving a huge hole close to the keel amidships. Hastily tossing a few provisions into a boat, the craft was launched and the men tumbled in just as the *Alexander* went down.

"Even worse than the predicament of the *Essex's* crew was that of these men from the *Alexander*, for one of their two boats had been stove and leaked like a sieve, and less than a day's supply of water and food had been secured. Regardless of this, however, the brave and reckless men started to row for land, but their troubles came to an unexpected and welcome end far sooner than they dared hope, for two days after leaving the scene of their adventures they were picked up by the ship *Nantucket*.

"And here it may be of interest to note that the mad whale which destroyed the *Alexander* was eventually captured and killed by another New Bedford ship. Five months after the whale had rammed the *Alexander* the *Rebecca Simms*, of New Bedford, took a whale, and, to the surprise of the men, pieces of planks and timbers were found sticking in his head, and when he was cut-in, two of the *Alexander's* irons were found in his body.

"Now we will take one more story of a ship

THE BOYS' BOOK OF WHALERS

being attacked by a whale and then turn to other tales. This last is interesting as it is probably the most recent of such disasters, and fortunately for the men, they were near land and all were saved. In 1910 the bark *Kathleen* of New Bedford was cruising in the West Indies to the east of the Leeward Islands. One of the boats had struck a whale, but the iron drew, and the great creature wheeled and rushed at the bark. The force of his impact smashed in the vessel's stout timbers, tore away several feet of planking and made such an enormous hole that the ship began to sink rapidly. There was no hope of saving the *Kathleen* and all hands, including the captain's wife who was on board, instantly took to the boats. Although the boats became separated in the darkness, land was not far distant and two reached shore in safety without loss of life and with little suffering, while the third was picked up by a passing vessel. Of the other two, one reached Barbados and the other Dominica. But we can imagine what their fate might have been had the *Kathleen* been sunk in mid ocean.

"When you asked about ships being attacked by whales I mentioned that cases were known of ships running onto sleeping whales. You might think, with good reason, that this would be a very rare occurrence; but, as a matter of fact, it is not, and a number of cases are known of vessels, and usually merchantmen at that, striking whales and being lost, for the result of striking a mountain of flesh and bone the size of a large whale is much the same as when striking a rock or reef, even though the whale suffers the most. Probably the earliest account of a vessel ramming a whale is that of a ship which ran into a whale during a storm in 1640. Although the vessel was not sunk, still the force of the blow stove in several planks, six timbers and a beam, broached two hogsheads of vinegar in the forehold and put the ship aback or 'in stays.'

"Some idea of the fearful resistance offered by a whale when hit by a moving ship may be gained from the report of the captain of the Scotch merchant ship *Cuban* which rammed a sleeping whale while bound to Demerara in 1857. The *Cuban* was a five-hundred-ton ship deeply laden and under full sail, and yet, when she hit the whale, her headway was instantly stopped and she was brought up as suddenly and completely as though she had struck the solid land.

"That whales when so hit are killed or injured is proved by the case of the ship *Herald of the Morning*, which, in 1859, put into Hampton Roads leaking badly and reported that a whale had been rammed near Cape Horn. The whale had been seen to spout blood as it disappeared, which is a sure sign of fatal injuries. In this case, the blow of the ship against the whale was so great that seven feet of the vessel's stem were started and the bobstay was carried away.

"Only a year after this, the *Eastern City* ran into a whale, and although this was a steamship and the whale was a mere baby only fifty feet in length, yet the steamer's cutwater was broken, while, in 1865, the schooner *Forest Oak* struck a whale between Boston and Nova Scotia with such force that every man on board was thrown flat to the decks and the foremast of the schooner was sprung and loosened.

"Still more recently, in 1873, the three-masted schooner *Watanga* struck a sleeping whale while making a speed of about seven knots and tore away the false stem, split the stem, started the planks, carried away the bowsprit and did so much damage that the vessel barely could be kept afloat until it reached port.

"In none of these cases was the ship actually lost; but back in March, 1796, the ship *Harmony* ran upon a whale off Brazil and sunk immediately, although the crew escaped in boats.

"Of all instances of ships being lost by striking whales, that of the *Union* is the most interesting and remarkable, as well the one of which we have the most detailed account.

"The *Union* set sail for Brazil from Nantucket on September 19th, 1807, and at ten o'clock at night on the first of October, while proceeding at about seven knots under easy sail, she unexpectedly ran onto a sleeping whale. So tremendous was the shock, that all on board thought the ship had struck a rock until the injured whale was seen. The ship was leaking badly and it was found that two timbers and the planking on the starboard bow had been staved in. Although the pumps were at once manned, yet the water continued to gain and two hours after striking the whale, orders were given to abandon the ship. As a heavy sea was running at the time and as there were sixteen men to man the three boats, one boat was abandoned and the men were divided between the other two, which were headed for the Azores about 600 miles away.

"The next morning, sails were rigged, but hardly was this done when the wind increased to a gale, the sails were destroyed and carried away, and to prevent the boats from becoming separated, they were lashed together and allowed to drift.

"As the men had been compelled to leave the ship hurriedly, an inadequate supply of water and very few provisions had been placed in the boats and the men were put upon slender rations of sixteen small cakes and three quarts of water for the whole number for each twenty-four hours. With starvation staring them in the face and suffering unspeakable torments from thirst, they kept on and rowed, sailed and drifted for seven days and eight nights until on October 9th they reached Flores Island and landed safely.

"In every one of these cases it has been assumed that the whales were sleeping upon the surface of the sea when struck, but it is not at all impossible that in more than one instance the whales merely happened to breach just at the moment when the ship was close upon them. Oddly enough, probably fewer whale ships were destroyed by fire than by any other cause although the vessels were soaked with oil and were highly inflammable, while the sparks and fire from the try works always jeopardized them. I know of but one record of a whaling ship lost by fire at sea, however; the story of the Providence ship *Cassander* and which bears the dark blot of almost inconceivable cruelty and inhumanity on the part of a merchant captain who refused to rescue the suffering, shipwrecked crew of the ill-fated vessel.

"Sailing on November, 1847, everything went well until fire was discovered on board on the first of May, 1848. The flames had started in the forehold among some barrels of tar near the foremast, and at the first cry of alarm, two African negroes of the crew jumped into the sea. Although life lines were thrown to them they refused to seize them and one was drowned before the second mate's boat could be lowered. This boat rescued the surviving negro, who then confessed that he and his dead comrade had started the fire, for fear that the whaleman would make them slaves, and that the other had shot himself before leaping overboard. The fire spread with amazing speed, owing to a half gale from the northwest, and soon realizing that it was impossible to save his ship, the captain ordered three boats lowered, and manned by the crew of twenty-three men.

"The location of the fire and the rapid spread of the flames had prevented the men from reaching the water-butts or provisions and there was but one biscuit and a gill of water for each day's rations per man. So stormy and windy was the weather, that the boat's sails could not be used and through the stupendous, breaking seas the men pulled the heavy boats for day after day until the seas calmed down, the wind fell and sails were set, when, four days after deserting their ship, a vessel was sighted. This proved to be a Spanish brig from Barcelona to Montevideo and with relieved minds and glad hearts the weary, starving, thirst-mad men drew alongside. Imagine their feelings, their utter hopelessness and their sufferings, when this inhuman captain,—this monster in man's form,—ordered the shipwrecked men off, and despite their pitiful appeals and prayers, refused even to take the boats in tow or to allow them a night's rest or even to supply them with water or food. Utterly unable to make headway against the seas and wind which again rose the men lashed their oars together as a sea-anchor and through the next twenty-four hours rode to this drag. On the afternoon of the second day a tremendous sea swamped the captain's boat, and while the brave fellows in the other boats saved all the men, their precious stores of food and water were lost, as well as their compass and sextant. But luckily the next morning dawned with light winds and the men had the blessed relief of a heavy shower. Refreshed by this, and with redoubled courage, the men again bent to their oars and three days later landed in Brazil.

"Although the sufferings of the whalers in their open boats were very great, yet there are many instances on record of whalemen preferring their tiny cockleshells to other ships, and although spoken, they often refused to be picked up, but after securing water and provisions,—and possibly their position,—they would continue on their voyage in the whaleboats and usually reached port in safety.

"On one occasion, a boat's crew was sighted by a Norwegian bark after they had been at sea in the open boat for nine days, and yet the men refused to go aboard as the bark was bound for England. On the following day, a whaling vessel saw them and when they went aboard they were so exhausted and dazed by privation and exposure that they did not realize they were on their own ship until two weeks after they were rescued. As recently as 1915, two boats were lost from the whaling schooner *John Manta* of New Bedford when off Hatteras. And although they saw several vessels, they stuck to their trusty whaleboat, and finally made New Bedford in safety. These men had been lost from their vessel through being towed out of sight by a whale. This was always one of the greatest of the whalemen's perils and probably more lives have been lost and more sufferings endured in this way than in any other. Very often, the men who were lost were picked up soon afterwards by other whale ships. Many times, too, the boats and crews were lost and never heard from again, while, in a few instances, they reached civilization, or were rescued by passing vessels, after incredible sufferings and endurance. To be towed out of sight of their ship was an everyday occurrence, and if the weather were fair and it was not late in the afternoon, it worried them little, for even if they could not see their ship, the lookouts on the mastheads could usually locate them, and they knew, moreover, that their captain would not desert them until he has searched the sea for days. But if night fell, if a storm arose or if they had been towed beyond sight of the lookouts on their ship the chances were all against them. Indeed, under such conditions, they were even worse off than men whose ships were sunk, burned or wrecked, for then the men at least could secure some provisions for their trip in the open boats, whereas, if lost when fast to a whale, only the meagre supply of biscuits and water, which are always in the boats, stood between them and the awful agonies of starvation and unquenchable thirst.

"It was largely due to this that so few boats' crews which were lost and were not rescued soon afterwards were ever heard from, and yet, a few did manage to survive the most fearful privations and reached land in the end. Such was the case with the men of the bark *Janet* of Westport.

"It was on the twenty-third of January in 1849 that one of the *Janet's* boats struck and ultimately killed a whale. A heavy sea was running and in attempting to tow their prize to their ship the boat was swamped and capsized. After a terrific struggle in the seas the men righted their boat, but all its contents, including the precious biscuits and water, the compass and even the lantern were lost. The whale had been killed late in the afternoon and night was approaching rapidly and although the crew made frantic endeavors to attract the attention of the ship to their plight they were unsuccessful. At last, realizing that no help could be expected, they lashed their oars across their water-logged boat, to prevent it from sinking, and worked it to the lee of the dead whale. Here they tried to empty the water from their craft, but without buckets or bailer, and with the huge seas breaking over the whale and themselves they found the feat impossible, and cutting loose from the carcass, started to work their water-filled boat towards the lights of their ship which were now dimly visible. Throughout the long, black night they labored, the seas constantly breaking over them and lashed into fury by the gale which had risen, and when at last the murky day dawned, they found all their Herculean efforts had been in vain and that they were steadily being carried further and further from the *Janet.*

"Giving up all hope of being able to reach their ship, but still undaunted, the men turned their boat about and endeavored to rest and renew some of their strength while drifting before the wind. All through that day and night they drifted at will of wind and waves, until, on the second morning, the wind died down and the men decided to capsize their boat and empty the water from it. In this they were partially successful, although in doing it one man was drowned while two others went mad,—crazed by the sufferings they had endured by being up to their armpits in water for forty-eight hours and without a morsel of food or a drop to drink in all that time. Without food or fresh water, with nothing but their oars, and with their boat still half full of water, their only hope lay in being picked up by some passing vessel or in the seemingly utterly impossible chance of reaching the nearest land which was Cocos Island off the South American coast and which they knew was over a thousand miles distant.

"Not a single man could exert strength enough to pull one of the huge ash oars, but by dogged persistence and superhuman efforts they managed to strip the light, wooden ceiling from the inside of their boat and with this they made a sort of wooden sail. Then, resigning themselves to their fate, the men floated before the wind across the trackless ocean, propelled at a snail's pace by this sorry makeshift.

"With no compass to guide them, thirst-mad and starving; steering by the sun during the day and by the stars at night, they sailed onwards under a broiling tropic sun for seven endless days. In all that time no shower brought a drop of water to their relief; no morsel of food passed their parched and swollen lips, not a sail gladdened their bloodshot, aching, half-closed eyes until, at last, driven almost to madness by their sufferings they drew lots to see who should be sacrificed to keep the rest alive, and one of the men was killed and devoured ere his flesh had grown cold. And then, as though the Almighty had taken pity upon them, came a heavy shower; but too late, for on the following day another man died. Again, on the ninth day, another blessed downpour furnished them with water and, as if sent by Providence, a dolphin actually leaped into their boat. Incredible as it may seem, miraculous as it may sound, yet nearly every day thereafter birds approached the boat and allowed the men to capture them, and thus fed by the hand of God, the men reached land on July 13th, after being twenty days adrift in their open boat.

"Landing upon Cocos Island, the men killed a wild hog, slaked their thirst with the clear, cold mountain water and two days after their arrival were picked up by the *Leonidas* of New Bedford. Can you wonder, that after such experiences; after men have been saved when their case seemed so hopeless; after food and water have been sent them direct from Heaven as it seemed, that the whalemen never gave up hope, that to the last breath they remained undaunted, indomitable, unafraid?

"And now how about the dangers, the losses and the adventures which fell to the lot of the whalers while chasing and killing the whale. This, to you, no doubt, seems the most dangerous part of the whaleman's life, and so it is. But the dangers of the actual chase threaten only a few men and seldom indeed were more than one or two members of a boat's crew lost when going on or killing a whale. Indeed, it is one of the most remarkable facts about whaling that so few men were seriously wounded or killed in their encounters with these monsters, for the boats were filled with keen-edged implements and weapons; fluke-spades, hatchets, knives, irons and lances, —and these were thrown helter-skelter among the struggling men when an enraged whale stove a boat or tossed it high in air with a sweep of his flukes. Then, in addition, there was the danger of the whizzing line always liable to tear a man to pieces or drag him deep beneath the sea, and while there are several instances of men being killed or injured in this manner, yet considering the vast number of whales killed and the army of men engaged in killing them, accidents of any kind were rare.

"One notable case, where the rushing line played havoc, was that of the mate's boat of the *Parker Cook* of Provincetown in 1850. The captain and chief mate both lowered and the boat-steerer of the latter's boat soon got two irons into a huge whale. As soon as he was struck, the whale sounded, breached under the boat, capsizing it, and as he did so, a kink of the line whipped about the boat-steerer's leg. Without an instant's hesitation, the whale then turned his attention to the captain's boat and attempted to seize it in his huge jaws, but was stopped in his rush and killed with a bomb-lance by the captain. When finally rescued, the boat-steerer was found to have his leg nearly severed from his body and he died from his injuries soon afterwards.

"Your friend Captain Ned has already told you the story of Jenkins; but here is a story almost as remarkable,—the story of a whaling captain who was tossed into the water as his boat was stove by a right whale. No doubt, had the creature been a sperm whale, the captain might have been seized in the whale's jaws and killed ere he had a chance to fight; but with the right whale he had only the flukes to avoid. This, however, was enough, for the huge creature turned on the swimming man, who, to save himself, dove under the whale and by swimming, dodging and diving strove to avoid the sweeping flukes and to escape from the crashing blows of the whale's head. Although buffeted about, the captain, by supreme efforts, managed to avoid a direct blow and though often driven far beneath the surface by the monster's strokes, he fought on for three-quarters of an hour while the boat hung off, unable to approach the maddened whale to strike him or to even rescue their skipper. Knowing that the tip of the right whale's nose is extremely tender and that the slightest injury to the nose will turn a whale of this kind, the captain drew his sheath knife and manœuvred to bury it in his assailant's nose. At last he succeeded and the whale beat a hasty retreat, leaving the exhausted captain to be rescued more dead than alive by his companions, but strangely enough scarcely injured. No doubt this whale, as well as those which rammed the ships and sunk them, was one of the 'mad' whales which were often reported by the whalers. Stories of such creatures were common and while they no doubt became exaggerated as they passed from mouth to mouth, yet there is no question that such creatures did exist,—monsters of unusual size, exceptional ferocity, incredible cunning and great courage;—veritable whale warriors which sought to destroy lives and boats whenever opportunity offered and were often successful and escaped death for years, despite every effort of the whalemen to take them.

"Such mad whales were easily identified when killed, for each ship which attacked them and left irons in their bodies left recognizable marks of the encounters, for all the ship's irons were marked and when a whale was found with irons in his body the fact was always entered in the logbook. If a ship whose irons were found had met with disaster or unusual adventures, the report of finding her irons was spread far and wide.

"Such was the case with the irons of the *Alexander* found by the *Barclay*, which I have already mentioned. Very often, too, a whale

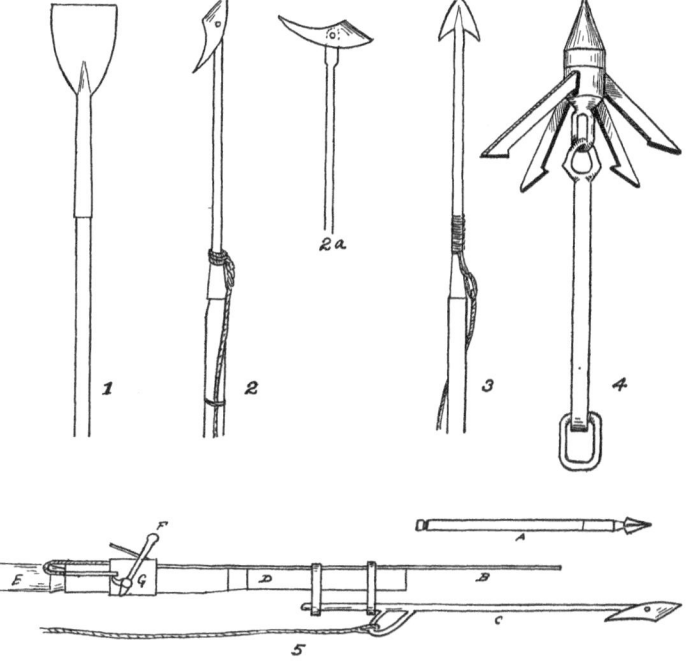

EXPLANATION — IMPLEMENTS AND WEAPONS USED IN WHALING

1 Blubber Spade
2 Iron or Harpoon used for whales
2a How the iron toggles or turns in the whale
3 Harpoon or iron used for porpoise
4 Iron fired from a gun by steam whalers
5 Darting gun and bomb lance combined

A Bomb lance fired from barrel
B Iron rod which fires gun when it comes in contact with whale
C Ordinary iron with line attached
D Gun barrel, about 20 in. long
E Iron pole fitted to brass butt of gun
F Lever for cocking gun
G Lock plate and firing pin

would be killed with irons in his body showing that he had traveled thousands of miles or that many years had elapsed since the irons had been buried in his flesh. For example, in 1815, Captain Paddok of the *Lady Adams* killed a whale and while cutting it in discovered an iron which he himself had thrown in a far distant part of the Pacific thirteen years before. Moreover, the discovery of irons in whales killed often proved of tremendous importance to the whalemen, and it was the fact that irons thrown and lost in Davis' Straits were found in whales taken in the Arctic, that proved the existence of an open Northwest Passage.

"So you readily can understand that if stories of a mad whale were spread among the whalemen and any ship's crew were fortunate enough to take him with the proofs in his body, it was not long before his capture was heralded throughout the whaling world.

"Here, for instance, is the report of the *Hector* of New Bedford which in October, 1832, lowered boats in chase of a large whale. Before they could come within striking distance, however, the whale turned and attacked the boats deliberately, staving one and tossing its crew into the sea. Pulling at topmost speed, the captain's boat hurried to the rescue, whereupon the fighting whale left the struggling men, and dashing at the oncoming boat, opened wide his jaws, seized the boat, and in a perfect paroxysm of fury, chewed and bit it to pieces. Then, throwing the destroyed boat to one side, the whale turned on the *Hector's* mate,—who was swimming for his life,—grasped him in his jaws and bit and chewed him horribly, finally letting him go badly wounded, but still alive.

"While the monster had been thus busy with the captain's boat and the unfortunate mate, the other boats had hurried to the scene and without hesitation struck the whale and after a long and desperate struggle succeeded in killing him. Towing him to the ship he was cut-in and in the process various irons were found in him which identified him as a famous 'mad' whale which had already destroyed many boats and men. Among these was the chief mate of the *Barclay,* who had been killed three months before and the lost irons of the *Barclay* were found in the creature's body.

THE BOYS' BOOK OF WHALERS

"Sometimes, oddly enough, the whales saved the men's lives,—though unconsciously,—as was the case when men under Captain Huntling struck a big sperm whale off the South American coast. This creature was also a 'mad' whale and like the one which fell to the *Hector's* men, he seized the boat in his jaws and chewed it to bits. As his attention was thus occupied, the other boat rescued the swimming men while two other boats went in on the whale and got irons into his side. Turning on these new enemies, the creature crushed both boats with right and left snaps of his stupendous jaw and left the twelve men struggling in the sea. As many of these could not swim, their only hope was to save themselves by climbing upon the infuriated whale's back, where, straddling his hump and with one of their number clinging to his side, they remained until rescued by a fourth boat.

"Six irons had now been lodged in his body, and fast to nine hundred fathoms of line, the whale was as full of fight as ever, and rushing at another boat he quickly destroyed it. Realizing the nature of their antagonist, the captain attempted to put an end to the whale by firing a bomb containing six ounces of powder into the whale; but instead of ending his career, the explosive appeared only to infuriate him the more and before the remaining boats could escape he dashed among them, tossed them aside, and with twelve hundred fathoms of line and seven irons disappeared with only the four ruined boats as the whalemen's reward for their desperate and unsuccessful battle.

"But the whales were not the only ferocious and dangerous things which the Yankee whalemen were called upon to fight. Many of the South Sea islands were discovered and first visited by the whalemen and while many of the natives were peaceful others looked upon strangers only as prospective meals. Such were the cannibals which attacked the ship *Awashonks* of Falmouth in October, 1835.

"It was on the fifth of October that the ship hove-to off Namarik Island in the Marshall group in order to recruit natives who were supposed to be friendly. About noon the first crowd of islanders came aboard, and little dreaming that there was the least danger, the captain, the chief mate and second mate went below to dinner, leaving the third officer in charge. As soon as the three had finished their meal, Mr. Jones went below and in about fifteen minutes returned and joined the others. At this time the crew were scattered over the ship, most of them being forward with one on watch, three aloft working on the rigging and one man at the wheel.

"Like a bolt from a clear sky, and without even a cry to warn the white men, the natives suddenly rushed for the blubber-spades and seizing the sharp steel implements fell upon the white men with savage yells. The first to fall was the helmsman, cut down with a spade; another spade beheaded the captain and the chief mate was slaughtered as he leaped into the forehatch.

"Striving to gain a place of safety on the bowsprit the second mate rushed forward, but was dragged back and clubbed to death. The third mate, seeing his fellows butchered, seized a spade and hurled it harpoon-like at an approaching savage who dodged it, and the mate, now the only living white man on deck, managed to reach the forehatch where the other members of the ship's crew had already hidden.

"Although they were afraid to go below and attack the men in the darkness, the natives crept forward, and having fastened down the hatches headed the ship towards the island with the idea of wrecking her. While this was going on the three men in the rigging, and who of course had escaped the savages, were not idle; but crawling down as near the deck as they dared, they cut the ship's braces which let the yards swing-to and the ship, thus beyond control of the natives, drifted away from the shore and towards the open sea.

"The crew and the third officer, imprisoned below decks, had also been busy in carrying out a desperate plan to save the ship and their own lives. Making their way aft to the cabin, where they obtained guns, the men, by firing through the windows, managed to keep the savages at a distance, while the third mate placed a keg of powder on the upper step of the companionway with a train of powder leading to the cabin.

"Touching this off, the keg exploded with a terrific report, killing and mutilating many of the natives, and so terrifying the others that when the crew dashed from the cabin to the deck every living native leaped overboard. At other times, however, the natives helped shipwrecked whalemen and saved their lives; as was the case when the crew of the *Canton* of New Bedford touched at one of the Ladrone islands during a trip in their boats which has no parallel in the history of the whaling industry.

"Moreover, the *Canton* was one of the few whaling ships which was lost through striking on a reef. In March, 1854, she struck an uncharted reef in the Pacific and went to pieces so rapidly in the heavy weather that the crew barely escaped in the four boats with but half a biscuit and half a pint of water per day for each man. Although there were islands within a comparatively short distance of the wreck, yet the weather was so bad, the seas so heavy and the wind so high, that the men were utterly unable to make the land and were obliged to head for the Ladrones where they arrived forty-five days after taking to the boats. The first island where they landed was uninhabited; but the men managed to capture a few fish and birds and again set forth, headed for Tinium Island thirty miles distant. Here the natives mistook them for pirates, but after considerable difficulty the men convinced the natives of their identity and they were then allowed to go ashore and were furnished with water and provisions. But the whalemen had no desire to remain upon this mid-Pacific island, and after a brief rest, again embarked in their tiny but staunch boats, and four days later, after a voyage of more than four thousand miles in their open boats, they reached Guam in safety.

"Even the savage cannibals were not the most dangerous foes with which the whalemen had to contend, however. Although mutinies were rare, yet several have been recorded which, for brutality and cold-blooded, ruthless butchery, have few equals in annals of the sea. One of the worst was that which took place on the *Globe* of Nantucket in 1824 and which was the more remarkable owing to the incredibly petty causes which brought it on. For over a year from the time the *Globe* had set forth from Nantucket in December, 1822, no trouble of any sort had been manifested on board the ship. The crew seemed contented and happy; they worked well, and the officers seemed well-liked and were neither brutal nor overbearing. Then, one day, while the crew was skylarking on the decks, one of the boat-steerers, a man named Comstock, was thrown by the third mate, Noah Fisher, in a friendly wrestling match. Exasperated by the taunts of the men at being defeated by Fisher, and enraged at being so easily worsted by the officer, the boat-steerer became so threatening and insolent that he was knocked down and slunk away, muttering threats to kill the mate. Little heed, however, was given to his threats, and the matter was entirely forgotten until the tragedy which transformed the peaceful ship to bloody shambles occurred.

"While the captain and chief mate were sleeping in the cabin on the night of January 25th, four men led by Comstock crept in and murdered both officers without even awakening them. Aroused by the sounds of the butchery, Lambert and Fisher,—the second and third mates—barricaded their cabin door and refused to open it at Comstock's demands when the boat-steerer fired a musket through the door, one of the bullets wounding the third mate in the mouth. The door was then smashed in and Comstock, in a futile blow at the second mate, lost his balance and fell inside the room, whereupon Lambert, with undaunted courage, seized the mutineer, who, after a short struggle, managed to escape. Fisher, in the meantime, although horribly wounded by the bullet in his mouth and suffering terribly, seized a bayonet and lunged at the boat-steerer who promised to spare the mates' lives if they would surrender.

"But no sooner had the officers thrown aside their weapons, than Comstock blew out Fisher's brains while one of his men pierced Lambert's body with a whale-lance.

"Then, with the ferocity of fiends incarnate, the mutineers mutilated their victims, and while Lambert, who was still alive, begged and screamed for mercy the two mates were tossed overboard.

"The ship was now in the hands of the mutinous murderers and was headed for the Malgrave Islands where Comstock and his men proceeded to loot her. Breaching a keg of rum, the mutineers soon became intoxicated, and during the drunken quarrel that arose over the division of the spoils, Comstock was murdered. In the confusion that followed his death, six of the men who had refused to take an active part in the mutiny, gained the ship unseen and cutting her cables, worked her out of the harbor and headed for the open sea. Reaching Valparaiso after a long and stormy trip, the six faithful whalemen delivered the *Globe* to the American consul and told of the mutiny and their escape.

"Placing the *Globe* in charge of Captain King, and sending her home, the authorities at once sent another ship with an armed crew to capture the marooned crew, but swift punishment already had been meted out to them and all but two men had been butchered by the natives when the vessel reached the island.

"Another famous whale ship mutiny, the cause of which was never known, was that of the New Bedford ship *Junior* which occurred in 1857. Sailing in July, the *Junior* rounded Cape Horn and spent the time until Christmas cruising in the Pacific. On Christmas Day, Captain Miller ordered spirits served to all his men, and leaving them apparently merry and enjoying themselves, went to his cabin.

"At daylight the next day, one of the crew,

Cyrus Plummer, accompanied by four men, armed themselves with muskets, made their way to the cabin and shot the sleeping officers, killing the captain instantly and riddling the mates with bullets; but not killing them outright. As the wounded third mate attempted to rise, he was cut down with a whale-spade, while the second and chief mates succeeded in escaping to the hold, although the latter had six musket balls in his body.

"As they returned to the deck after their bloody deed, the mutineers were met by such of the crew who remained faithful; but finding themselves outnumbered, and realizing the fate in store for them if they resisted, the loyal men gave in and joined the others. Now that the crew was in control of the ship they spent several days in drinking and merrymaking until it dawned upon them that, without the officers, they were helplessly at the mercy of the ocean, as not a single man in the crew understood navigation.

"As their murderous fury subsided, and as the men grasped the predicament they were in, they shouted into the hold to the wounded, suffering officers promising to spare their lives if they would navigate the ship. Nearly dead with loss of blood and their uncared-for wounds and suffering from thirst and lack of food the two mates dragged themselves forth, and under the pistols of the mutineers, navigated the *Junior* to within twenty miles of the Australian coast.

"Here, the mutineers rifled the ship of all valuables and provisions and taking to the boats headed for the land; but their freedom was of short duration and eight of them were promptly caught and hung. Before their execution they had decency enough to make a written confession in which they exonerated the other members of the crew, while the ringleader, Plummer, turned State's evidence and thus saved his worthless neck.

"From such dastardly deeds as these it is pleasant to turn to the accounts of adventures wherein the whalemen performed brave and worthy deeds for the sake of their fellow men. And such occurrences were far more common than mutinies, for the whalers, although rough, were, as a rule, most resourceful and brave men, accustomed to taking enormous risks and never hesitating to attempt tasks which to others would appear impossible. Indeed, a volume might be written on the deeds of prowess performed by whalemen, but one of them was so unique and well carried out that it will interest you.

"Early in April, 1771, two Nantucket whale sloops were anchored in the harbor of Abaco Island in the Bahamas when a vessel was sighted with signals for help showing at her mastheads.

"With their customary willingness to help, one of the boats was lowered and the captain of one of the whalers pulled to the approaching vessel and climbed aboard. The instant he gained the deck he was thunderstruck at having a pistol placed at his head while, in gruff tones, he was ordered to pilot the ship to the inner harbor or be killed. With the quick wit of a resourceful man, the whaleman replied that he would be willing to do so but was a stranger to the island and did not know the channel, adding that one of his men knew the way in. He was then ordered to point out this man who was called aboard and threatened as had been the captain, and knowing resistance would be useless, he guided the ship into the harbor. But this man was no more of a fool than his skipper, and realizing that something was wrong, he brought the vessel to anchor where a point of land separated her from the two whaling sloops. The two whalemen were then released and proceeded to their ship where the two Yankee skippers held a hurried conference as to the best method of outwitting and capturing the crew of the strange vessel whom they were convinced were either pirates or mutineers, as the two whalemen had noticed that a man was held under an armed guard in the cabin.

"The two skippers soon decided upon the course to follow and sent an invitation to dinner to the captain of the strange ship. The invitation was quickly accepted and the so-called captain of the stranger soon arrived accompanied by his boatswain and bringing with him the unarmed man who had already been seen in the cabin. Scarcely had they stepped on board, before they were surrounded, seized and securely bound by whalers who had been hidden awaiting a signal from their skipper.

"The whalemen then learned, from the man

who had been held a captive, that he was the real commander of the vessel which was from Bristol, Rhode Island, and had sailed from that port for Africa. There he had taken on a cargo of slaves, had carried them to the West Indies and had set sail for home, when his crew mutinied, seized the ship and decided to become pirates. As no member of the crew understood navigation, they had spared his life and that of the mate, keeping the latter a prisoner in the hold and compelling their former captain to navigate the vessel under guard.

"Telling the pirate boatswain that if he would return to his ship, free the former mate and aid the whalemen in recapturing the vessel, they would try to have him pardoned for his part in the mutiny, they told him he was free to go. But before he left they warned him that within two hours' sail they knew where a British man-o'-war was at anchor, and that if he did not do as he was told they would sail to the warship, secure an armed force and return and capture the pirates.

"As the whalemen had expected, the pirate boatswain made no sign of complying with their orders and one of the Nantucket sloops at once hoisted sail and stood out from the harbor. As they approached the mutineers' ship, the latter hurried about, shifting their guns to the port side of their ship where the whaling vessel was about to pass and preparing to sink her as soon as she was within range. But the Yankee skipper was not to be caught napping and when almost within gunshot, he suddenly jibed and swept past the other side of the ship and out of range long before the furious mutineers could move their cannon across their decks. Leaving the harbor, the little Nantucket sloop sailed out of sight and standing off and on beyond a point of land, waited several hours and headed back towards the harbor with a signal at the masthead as if they had spoken a man-o'-war, and with red cloths wrapped about the crew to resemble the red coats of British marines.

" Seeing the sloop sailing boldly towards them, and fully believing that the whalemen had fulfilled their threats, the mutineers tumbled into their boats, and pulling with all haste to the shore, where they sought to escape, but were quickly captured by the aid of the inhabitants.

"With the mutineers safely secured and the released mate in charge of a crew of whalemen, the Nantucket vessels convoyed the ship to Nassau, where the whalemen were paid a reward of $2,500 for what they had done, and the leader of the mutineers was hung.

"And now, that we have had stories of so many of the adventures of the whalemen, so many tragedies of the sea, so many accounts of disasters and escapes, perhaps you will be interested in a brief description of the greatest disaster that ever occurred to the whaling fleets of New England. Of all the perils of the sea which menaced the whaling ships, the greatest was that of being crushed in the Arctic ice, and more ships were lost in that way than by all other accidents put together. Twice, in 1871 and in 1876, whole fleets of ships were destroyed in this way, and while the loss in 1876 was large,—twenty vessels being crushed,—yet it was nothing as compared to the catastrophe of five years earlier when thirty-two ships were destroyed at one time with a monetary loss of over two million dollars to New Bedford alone and which left over twelve hundred persons shipwrecked on the Arctic ice fields.

THE BOYS' BOOK OF WHALERS

It was by far the greatest blow the industry ever suffered and it stands out as one of the most marvelous, if not the most remarkable, of all known maritime disasters, for not a single life was lost, despite the dangers and rigors of the Arctic and the fact that twelve hundred and nineteen souls,—men, women and children,—were carried in open whaleboats for nearly one hundred miles through ice-laden, storm-beaten, freezing seas in order to reach safety.

"It was in May, 1871, that the Arctic whaling fleet gathered south of Cape Thaddeus waiting for the closely-packed ice to open and permit them to make their way to the more northerly grounds. By the middle of June the vessels had reached Behring Straits, and through July the ships were busy whaling until during the latter part of the month, when the ice drifted and the fleet headed east, following the ice through open leads until within a short distance of Icy Cape. Here a few of the ships anchored, as the ice still prevented them from reaching the Blossom Shoal grounds, but by the sixth of August there was clear water and several of the vessels set sail and a few days later nearly all of the fleet was north of the shoals and had worked to the northeast of Wainwright Inlet, where eight vessels anchored or made fast to the ice and all were busy whaling. But on the eleventh of August the wind shifted suddenly and set inshore, nipping several of the boats which were cruising for whales, and forcing the ships to get under way. Several of the boats were stove, but all were saved by pulling them on the ice close inshore, and on August 13th the vessels reached Point Belcher and waited for a northeast wind to carry off the ice. But instead of coming from that quarter, as they expected, the wind came from the west, driving the ice ashore and forcing the ships up a narrow strip of water less than half a mile in width and close to the land. Here they were fast, but as whales were everywhere in the open water, the chase continued, the blubber being cut-in at the edge of the ice-pack and carried over it to the ships.

"On August 25th the long-looked-for northeaster arrived, driving the pack eight miles off the shore, and the Eskimos advised the whalemen to make the most of the open water while they had a chance. The whalemen, however, re-

THE BOYS' BOOK OF WHALERS

mained to capture whales and four days later the wind shifted, the ice again came driving inshore, and several ships were caught in the pack.

"The first loss to the fleet occurred on September 2d, when the *Comet* was crushed, her crew escaping to the other ships. On the seventh of the month the bark *Roman* was caught and crushed; the next day the famous old *Awashonks* was destroyed and the crews of the ships, realizing their predicament, set to work sheeting their boats and building up the gunwales to protect them from the ice which now was a vast, unbroken field for eighty miles.

"It was now hopeless to expect any of the imprisoned ships to escape. Each day more vessels were stove or crushed; the ice,—grinding and crushing together by the force of the gale and seas,—rose and buckled in miniature mountains, lifting the big whale ships high in air, toppling them on their sides; tossing them about like toys and splitting their stout timbers and planks like pipe stems. Knowing that their only hope lay in reaching the ships further south, a boat was sent out to search for the other vessels and upon their return reported that six ships, besides the *Arctic*, were still clear and would wait to receive the fugitives if they abandoned their ships at once. There was nothing else to be done, so the boats were provisioned, the flags were set union down on the doomed ships, and loaded with men and a number of women and children, the flotilla set forth on the brave but unspeakably dangerous attempt to reach the ships beyond the ice-pack and eighty miles away. At the end of the first day a landing was made on a narrow beach at the foot of some sand hills and here the boats were turned up and transformed into shelters for the women and children by stretching canvas over them. On the second day Blossom Shoals were reached and the fugitives caught sight of the waiting vessels beyond a tongue of ice five miles distant.

"But to any one but a whaleman it would have appeared suicidal to attempt to reach them. The seas were running mountain high, and a terrific gale was blowing, while the spray froze instantly wherever it touched. Sheltered by the protecting strip of ice, the boats constantly shipped water; but as soon as this was passed every sea broke into the boats, provisions were soaked, the occupants were drenched to the skin in the icy brine, and to prevent the boats from sinking, they were compelled to bail for their lives. So terrific was the gale, so tremendous the seas, that the huge anchor chain of the *Arctic* was snapped as if mere rope yarn. And yet the tiny cockleshells, with their precious, human freight, bore on;—now hidden from the anxious watchers on the ships between the huge green billows; anon carried skyward on their foaming crests; but steadily drawing ever nearer to safety,—the women never complaining, the men never faltering until, without the loss of a single soul, the staunch whaleboats weathered the Arctic tempest and the twelve hundred and nineteen human beings reached the waiting ships and safety. Surely might the whalemen be forever proud of such a record of heroism, courage and seamanship!"

CHAPTER VIII

"YOU might think that the lot of the whalemen who cruised in tropical and semitropical seas in pursuit of sperm whales and visited palm-fringed islands abounding in luscious fruits, fresh vegetables and friendly natives was far preferable to the life of the arctic whalers who cruised in the frozen polar seas, whose ships picked their way cautiously and in ever constant peril among ice-floes and icebergs and who spent the long, bitterly cold, arctic winters in the desolate ice-bound land. Frozen fast in some bay or sound, the whale ships remained throughout the winter and not only through one, but often several winters, only returning when at last the ship's hold was filled with oil and bone.

"But oddly enough, the life on an arctic whaler held many attractions and appealed far more strongly to many men than sperm whaling or ocean cruising.

"In the first place, the work was easier if no less dangerous, it was varied and there were constant changes in scene and occupation; the food was better and for long months during the winter there was practically nothing for the men to do but amuse themselves and pass the time as they saw fit.

"Once the ship was in the grip of the ice and frozen in until spring, whaling of course was out of the question and while there were seals and walrus to be caught through the ice, polar bears and musk-oxen to be hunted, yet this was mere sport and recreation compared to hunting, killing, cutting in and trying out the whales.

"Moreover, the men had company, for the Eskimos always gathered about a whale ship, not only because they could earn reward in the form of trinkets, tools, food and supplies in return for their aid in whaling and in exchange for bone, hides, skin and meat which they brought in, but because they were sure of having a glorious time and breaking the dull monotony of their lives by visiting and being visited by the whale men. Often they would come from far distant points, traveling in their tiny skin kyaks or by dog sledge and camping near the whale ship until quite a good sized village had grown up. In the winter they built their igloos of snow and ice and in the summer erected their skin tents. And they were always welcomed by the whalemen and were well treated and fairly dealt with. In fact, the whalers depended in large measure upon their dusky skinned Eskimo friends for the success of their trips to the arctic.

" The Eskimos were skilled boatmen and whalers; they knew where schools of right whales or bowheads were to be found, they could supply the ships with meat, salmon, ducks, fish and other food, they provided the skins and made the fur garments which the whalemen used and they brought in walrus ivory, seal skins, musk-ox and bear hides, white and blue fox pelts and many other trophies of the chase which were frequently of far greater value than the catch of oil or bone.

" Many of the Eskimo men were regularly employed by whaling ships year after year and, by some intuition or sixth sense, seemed to know just when a ship would arrive and where they would find it and would be on hand ready and waiting to join the crew and go a-whaling.

"Another reason which led whaling captains and ship owners to seek the arctic grounds was that a ship could carry a smaller crew and could save many dollars in the north. With only enough men to handle the ship, or perhaps one boat, they could sail to the Arctic and there take on a gang of Eskimos. These men were hard workers, they were absolutely fearless where boat work or whaling was concerned, they knew how to handle the irons and lances, they were thoroughly familiar with the habits of the whales and they were adepts at stripping off the blubber, cutting out and dressing the bone and boiling the blubber.

"Moreover, they worked for practically nothing and even the poorly paid and systematically robbed derelicts who formed the crews of whaling ships were paid fortunes in comparison to the wages of the Eskimos, for these people had no use for money—they could not spend it if they had it—they had no idea of the value of their services or the pelts and hides brought in and would only accept trade goods in exchange for their work and their products. The cheapest and simplest things would serve for their needs and the arctic whalers always carried a large stock of beads, bright colored calico, hatchets, knives, cheap tobacco and pipes, mirrors, geegaws, scrap iron and files. An Eskimo, like a primitive Indian, only values an article in proportion to how much he needs it. If he wants arrow or harpoon tips, some scrap sheet iron and a file are worth more in his eyes than any other article with an intrinsic value many times greater. If his wife or wives wanted beads or calico a polar bear skin or a dozen fox pelts which were superfluous at the time were not worth as much as fifty cents' worth of the coveted articles. If the Eskimo had an ancient muzzle loading musket but no ammunition, powder and lead were ample payment for weeks of toil. But there was one trade article which the whalers never took to the Eskimos and that was soap. With all their good points the Eskimos are unspeakably filthy and no one but the grease-soaked whalemen accustomed to the dirt, grime and stench of whaling could have hobnobbed with them for months at a time save through dire necessity.

"But such matters never troubled the whalemen, even if they ever thought of it, and because the Eskimos never bathed nor washed and when the layer of filth upon their skins became too

THE BOYS' BOOK OF WHALERS

thick, removed it by plastering on blood and then scraping it off when dry, meant nothing in the eyes of the whalemen. Indeed, I doubt if the whalers had much more use for soap than their dark-skinned companions, for there were no facilities for either bathing or washing; the only water available was obtained from melted snow and the men wore the same clothes and furs for months at a time without ever removing them. Nevertheless, or rather I might say because of this, they got along on very friendly terms with the Eskimos and had gay and hilarious times. Games and competitions in strength, wrestling, jumping and other athletic sports were held on the ship's deck, dances and entertainments were given and holidays, such as Christmas, Thanksgiving, Washington's Birthday, etc., were celebrated in fine style.

"The arctic bound whaler timed his ship's departure so that he reached the northern seas—the Straits of Belle Isle if headed for the Hudson's Bay district or Behring Straits if for the western arctic grounds,—just as the ice was breaking up and the channels opening in spring. Skilled and daring in navigating the ice-filled seas, the whalemen worked their ships between the floes and bergs and among the pack ice until, by the time summer came on, they were well north and in the desolate seas and straits far beyond the last outposts of civilization. Here, at some well known point, they would pick up their Eskimo crew and cruise about for whales. Sometimes too they would anchor close to shore, establish try works on land and go a-whaling in their small boats accompanied by their Eskimo friends. This was a favorite method in Hudson's Bay and was thoroughly enjoyed by the men, for to sail a light, swift whale boat on a hunt for whales is not by any means a hard or unpleasant job.

"Then, when the short summer began to wane, the ship was prepared for the long, bitterly cold winter. Sails were unbent, spars sent down, the ship was secured in some sheltered cove or inlet and a rough board house was constructed over the decks to serve as the home of the crew during the frigid winter night while the ship was gripped in the relentless ice that would stretch away for hundreds of miles covering sea and land.

"Within this big deck house, bunks were arranged, tables erected and stoves set up and when at last the ice began to cover the sea and bay and the sea birds, ducks and geese had all departed for their winter homes in the south and even the hardy caribou and musk-oxen moved southward the whalers were snug and comfortable. If all went well the ship would be frozen in gradually and as the ice thickened she would be lifted bodily, forced up by the pressure, for the whale ship's massive oak ribs and planks were designed and built to withstand anything. At times, however, matters went far from well and a sudden pinching of ice or an inshore wind or storm or a cataclysm of the frozen mass would break the strongest ship as though she were an egg-shell. Perhaps it might leave her fit for habitation until the spring thaws came and the ice broke up, or again it might utterly destroy her. In the latter case the whalemen were willy-nilly compelled to desert the ship and wait ashore in hastily constructed camps until the sea was again open. Then by whale boat and canoe or by sledge if necessary they would journey countless miles over the bleak and dismal land to some other whale ship of whose whereabouts they knew. And more than once it happened that the other ship also had suffered and both crews were marooned for a year or more until rescued by some other whaler. Sometimes the newcomer would be a Scotch or Scandinavian vessel just starting on a voyage and several years might elapse before the shipwrecked men, on their new-found home, would be carried to Scotland or Norway and later work their way home after they had been mourned as dead for years.

"But as a rule, the whale ships suffered but little from the ice. Even if badly stove or crushed they would frequently manage to get home safely, for whale ships will stand an incredible amount of rough usage and although they might leak like a sieve the whalers manage to get them into port at last. One whaling captain who has spent many years in the Arctic told me of how his ship was once pinched in the ice until her decks actually buckled up above the bulwarks, and yet, after the ice gave way, she settled back and was sailed home to New London apparently little the worse. But in her log, in terse matter-of-fact sentences and misspelled words, you can read between the lines and see the heroic measures, the unremitting toil, the ceaseless vigilance and the almost superhuman endurance which were required to bring the old ship from the far-off Arctic down through ice-filled, tumultuous seas to Long Island Sound. Day and night the men labored steadily at the old-fashioned pumps, sail had to be shortened in order to avoid straining her already cracked and splintered planks and timbers, every time she met with heavy seas her seams opened and the water poured in almost as fast as the men could pump it out and over and over again it actually gained on them and it was a race for life to see if she could be kept afloat. Luckily, however, an old whale ship is so thoroughly grease soaked that it takes a large crack to allow much water to enter while the exuding oil makes a slick all about her and prevents the seas from breaking. Also, the cargo of oil is not injured by water and is buoyant and so, although the ship barely crawled along under her reduced rigging and often drifted far off her course, yet the men kept doggedly on. Any merchant ship's crew and captain would have abandoned her at once and would have taken to their boats rather than take the slim chance of keeping their ship afloat. But not so the hardy whalemen. They had worked hard and had been through three winters in the arctic to secure the full cargo of oil and the many tons of whalebone in the hold and the great bales of bear, musk-ox and fox hides worth thousands of dollars and as long as the battered old hulk would stay on top of the sea they had no intention of leaving her, but manfully stuck to their ship with success at last when, half filled with water, leaking at every seam, weather-beaten and gray, but without a man lost she sailed triumphantly into New London harbor.

"The captain of this same ship was a very observant and unusually wide-awake man and interested in many matters aside from whaling. He brought back large collections of bird skins, mammals, birds' eggs, minerals and other specimens for the museums of the country; he discovered and described a new and hitherto unknown tribe of Eskimos dwelling on one of the unexplored islands in Hudson's Bay and he knew enough to secure a good collection of their handiwork and a fairly complete vocabulary of their language. Not only that, but having a small camera on his ship he managed to secure many

THE BOYS' BOOK OF WHALERS

very valuable and interesting photographs which were developed under almost insurmountable difficulties.

"His logs are most fascinating reading, for he did not confine himself to matters of seamanship, statements of catches, remarks about the weather, etc., but filled pages with descriptions of Eskimo life and habits, stories of hunts, tales of his adventures and even found space and time to write down translations of innumerable Eskimo fairy tales and folk-lore together with crude illustrations of the stories drawn by the Eskimos themselves. Indeed, his logs are of tremendous scientific value and for this reason were acquired by one of our largest museums.

"In one of these logs too you may get a very good insight into the life of the whalers in the arctic, for he describes in minute detail all the games and contests of the Eskimos and a Christmas celebration. No doubt, the rough whalemen took as much pleasure and as keen a delight in this as do children with their Christmas trees at home, for while a tree was out of the question the resourceful whalers built a most fitting substitute in the form of a miniature whaling ship with its yards and masts as gaily decorated with candles, colored ribbons and trinkets as any one could desire while its hull served to hold the presents intended for both the whalemen and their Eskimo guests. And no one was overlooked, every one had some present. For the Eskimo men there were pipes, tobacco, matches, lead, shot, powder, bullets, knives, files, iron for spear heads and even pine boards which are valued highly in a land where the only wood and timber are drift wood from old wrecks. For the Eskimo women, there were needles and thread, thimbles, cheap jewelry, beads, scissors, pins and many other trinkets. The whalemen had ditty-bags with buttons, needles, thread, etc., jumpers and overalls, socks, caps, tobacco and pipes, jack-knives and other useful articles, while the Eskimos, not to be outdone and catching the spirit if not the significance of the day, gave their whalemen friends reindeer moccasins, fur coats and trousers, carved walrus tusks and other samples of their handiwork. All these were distributed by the big captain, garbed in his Eskimo suit of white bear skin and with a huge false beard of raveled rope yarn to make him appear still more like Santa Claus. And as no Christmas would be complete without the kiddies, the round-faced, slant-eyed little Eskimos found Santa had not forgotten them, but handed them dolls, jumping-jacks, mouth-organs and other toys.

"Then, as a fitting end of the day, long plank tables were spread with roast wild duck and goose, roast venison, ptarmigan, plum duff and plenty of potatoes and tinned vegetables while, for the special benefit of their Eskimo guests, the men had provided such delicacies as seals' blubber, walrus tongues, whale steak and lard which to an Eskimo is a far greater dainty than plum pudding or pumpkin pie.

"And when at last all had dined and could eat no more the crew brought out a battered accordion and an old fiddle and there, with the biting arctic gales howling about the ice-bound ship and piling up mountains of snow and with the mercury in the thermometer out of sight somewhere around 50° below zero the rough, good-natured New England whalemen and the Eskimos danced and sang and made as merry as ever a Christmas gathering in old New London town.

"Such was the brighter side of the whaleman's life and at times he showed that he was not blind to the finer and higher things; that he loved romance and was willing to throw his lot with the under dog. Indeed, I could relate scores of instances where the whalemen went out of their way to help some one or to have a hand in some undertaking just for the pure enjoyment of the adventure. One of the most romantic deeds ever undertaken by the whalers was the liberation of Fenian prisoners confined in Australia. The ship selected for this hair-brained and yet successful expedition was the New Bedford whaling ship *Catalpa* and aside from those intimately connected with the true purposes of the voyage all thought she was fitting for an ordinary whaling cruise. The prime mover of the scheme was John W. Goff, who afterwards became Justice of the Supreme Court, but the active leader was Mr. Thomas Brennan, who died in New York in November, 1915, and was the last survivor of this remarkable voyage during which the old ship and her company underwent adventures which might well form the basis of a most thrilling and romantic novel.

"The *Catalpa,* under Captain Anthony, cleared from New Bedford April 29th, 1875, and was not heard from until a year later, when safe and sound, she entered New York harbor bearing the six Fenians who had been sentenced to life imprisonment in Australia.

"Leaving New Bedford the ship, as usual with whalers, made for the Azores where she was to be joined by Mr. Brennan, who was also to put aboard a case of firearms in addition to a large sum of money, for he and his fellows were prepared to resort to force if milder methods failed and the whalemen looked forward expectantly to a lively time. Unfortunately, however, Mr. Brennan's ship, the *Gazelle,* was delayed and did not reach the Azores until the *Catalpa* had cleared and Mr. Brennan found that he would be compelled to go to England in order to join his ship. His predicament was a most serious one, for the only vessel leaving for England—the *Selbourne* —refused to take him and his companions, the captain claiming he thought them criminals trying to evade justice. But notwithstanding that Mr. Brennan was himself a political fugitive from England, he and his friends stowed away on the *Selbourne*, forsook the ship when near Liverpool and were rescued in an almost drowning state by a chance small boat.

"Reaching London secretly he conferred with friends and learned that the *Catalpa* was off Australia awaiting the arms and Mr. Brennan's party. After innumerable adventures the indomitable leader managed to reach Australia and on a secluded portion of the coast at a place called Rotten Nest, twenty-eight miles from Freemantle he at last joined the old whaling ship *Catalpa*.

"But their real troubles and adventures had just commenced. They were compelled to march the twenty-eight miles to Freemantle, where the prisoners were confined, through the bush, and after rescuing the Fenians from prison retrace their way to the coast. It was a daring, reckless, apparently impossible undertaking and no fiction ever written could equal the exciting incidents, the narrow escapes and the adventures actually encountered on that Quixotic trip. But despite all, the prisoners and their rescuers at last were safely aboard the whale ship. Then, scarcely was the *Catalpa* under way before she was chased by a ship, the *Georgette,* manned by the British authorities and equipped with artillery.

"The old *Catalpa* was a mere snail compared to the speedy *Georgette* and was soon overhauled and commanded to surrender by the British, but those on the *Georgette* did not know the New England whalemen's characters and instead of heaving to and surrendering Captain Anthony coolly pointed to the American flag flying from his gaff and politely invited the British to 'fire away.'

"Had the pursuers accepted his invitation the story of the *Catalpa* might have been a very different one, but the British commander seemed rather doubtful about the advisability of firing on an American ship and bringing on international complications for the sake of six Fenian prisoners and finally deciding the whalemen had the trump cards he reluctantly shifted his helm and put back, leaving the dingy old whaler to go wallowing on her way towards the distant United States and freedom.

"Of course it was pure bluff on the part of Captain Anthony, for the *Catalpa* caught redhanded was little more than a pirate and the

British authorities were wholly within their rights, no matter what public sympathy might say, but on many an occasion that same 'Yankee bluff' won the day when the whalemen were in a tight place.

"For years after the war of 1812, during which the whaling industry suffered tremendous losses there was always hard feeling between the Yankees and the Britishers whenever they met. Once, so the traditions in whaling circles say, an overbearing British officer and a New Bedford whaling captain had a heated argument and as words led to words and insult to insult the Englishman finally demanded satisfaction and challenged the weather-beaten old skipper to a duel. Being the challenged party, the whaleman had the choice of weapons whereupon he promptly announced 'Harpoons at ten paces' and the discomfited British officer promptly apologized and withdrew his challenge.

"Later, during the Civil War, the whalemen also suffered severely, for their slow and unarmed ships fell easy victims to the Confederate cruisers and privateers. The famous *Shenandoah* in particular wrought havoc among the whaling fleet and as a usual thing the whalemen, to save their lives, surrendered without other resistance than cursing the 'Rebs' vociferously and fluently.

"But now and then the Confederate officers caught a tartar, as in the case of Captain Thomas G. Young of the Fairhaven bark *Favorite*. The *Shenandoah* had been cruising in the North Pacific, destroying whaling vessels right and left and having her own way, when, after sinking five ships in Behring Straits she came upon a fleet of whalers aiding the *Brunswick* which had been crushed in the ice. At sight of the Confederate privateer the whalemen were panic stricken and were ready to surrender, but not so old Skipper Young. Loading every firearm aboard, charging his darting guns and bomb lances and placing irons, lances and spades within reach the old fellow prepared to resist to the end and standing on his cabin roof shook his fist at the rebels and defied them to do their worst. As the Confederates sent a boat to board the *Favorite* the bronzed-faced New Englander looked so fierce and determined that the boarding officer realizing it was no mere bluff very wisely turned about and retreated to his ship. Realizing they had a new type of Yankee skipper to deal with, the captain of the *Shenandoah* trained a gun on the *Favorite* and sent a shot crashing through the bark's hull. But even this warning of the hopelessness of resisting failed to make the whaleman quail. Instead, he grew more defiant, cursed the Confederates as a pack of blackguards, thieves, pirates and cowards and when his own officers,—realizing their position—remonstrated with him, he replied with a fervid oath that he would die happy if he could only shoot Waddell, the *Shenandoah's* commander.

"Thinking their skipper had gone stark mad the mates secretly removed the caps and charges from the firearms and to save themselves took to the boats, leaving the savage old skipper alone upon the cabin of the *Favorite*. Not wishing to destroy him in cold blood, Captain Waddell thereupon sent a boat in charge of an officer to the whale ship with orders to make Captain Young a prisoner and to haul down his flag which still flaunted defiantly at the mast. The instant the Confederate set foot on deck Captain Young seized a musket, aimed at the enemy and pulled

THE BOYS' BOOK OF WHALERS

the trigger and then, finding the weapon useless, cast it aside and leaped upon the officer with clenched fists.

"To protect himself, the Confederate drew his pistol and threatened to shoot, but even this could not check the whaleman, who rushed at the other crying, 'Shoot and be damned.' At this instant, however, the armed men from the *Shenandoah's* boat had gained the deck and piling upon the whaleman overpowered him and made him a prisoner.

"One would have thought that the gallant and heroic whaleman would have won the respect and admiration of even the Confederates and that he would have been treated as he deserved, but to the disgrace and shame of the rebels, Captain Waddell ordered the brave old skipper placed in irons, he took possession of all the whaleman's private and personal property and treated him in a more brutal and inhumane manner than if he had been a common malefactor or convict."

CHAPTER IX

"WE were reading a magazine last night and it said something about ambergris," said Rob, when the boys reached the museum. "In the story the hero found a lump of the stuff and sold it for a fortune. Can you tell us what ambergris is and if it really is valuable?"

"And the story spoke of killing whales with guns and steamers," put in Harry. "I've heard of steam whalers and you have spoken of 'bomb-lances,' but we'd like to know more about such things, even if they're not as interesting and exciting as the old-time whalers."

"Very well," smiled the good-natured curator, "I'll try to answer your questions and tell you all I can about the modern steam whalers and their methods, but I'm afraid it's not very much. Steam whaling is such a matter-of-fact, business proposition that there is little of romance, adventure or danger in it, and it never appealed to me. But to answer your first questions about ambergris.

"Ambergris is a most peculiar substance, and for a great many years its origin was a mystery. Sometimes it was found floating upon the sea; at other times cast upon beaches, and occasionally it was discovered within the bodies of whales. But as bits of cuttlefish beaks were sometimes found in it, and as scientists learned that sperm whales fed upon these creatures, they deduced that there was a very close connection between the origin of the ambergris and the food of the sperm whales. Finally it was discovered that the ambergris is a disease growth caused by an accumulation of indigestible portions of cuttlefish or squids which lodge in the whale's intestines, and some of the largest masses of the substance ever taken have been secured by dissecting the whales. In appearance it is grayish, greasy and porous—looking a good deal like old water-soaked bread,—and as it is very light it floats upon the surface of the sea. It has a peculiar, rather sickish, odor and its value lies in the fact that it possesses the remarkable quality of holding, or absorbing, odors. Owing to this, it is largely used in manufacturing perfumes, while in China it is used as medicine. It is worth considerably more than its weight in gold, but is not as valuable as many suppose and as stories would have us believe. At times it has been sold for as much as one thousand dollars a pound, although its average value is from three to five hundred dollars; but as ambergris is so light it takes a large lump to weigh a pound. Nevertheless, many a poor sailor and whaleman has made a moderate fortune by finding a mass of ambergris, and not infrequently the ambergris brought back by a whaling ship has been worth more than the entire cargo of oil.

"I cannot say what the largest mass of ambergris ever found weighed, but I have a report here of all the ambergris secured by whaling vessels for a period of seventy-three years—from 1841 until 1914. According to this the largest quantity brought in by any one ship was 983 pounds by the bark *Splendid,* of New Zealand, in 1883. The next largest find was 800 pounds brought in by the schooner *Watchman,* of Nantucket, in 1858. Following this are lots weighing 214 pounds from the schooner *Antarctic,* of Provincetown, in 1887; 208 pounds by the bark *Elizabeth,* of Westport, in 1870, and 200 pounds from the Azores in 1910. There are several more records of over 100 pounds, but most of the lots weighed only ten or twelve pounds, the smallest amount being three pounds found by the bark *Morning Star*, of New Bedford, in 1906. The grand total of all amounts to 4,388 pounds, or about sixty pounds a year, the total value probably being about two million dollars,—a goodly sum to be sure, but when distributed over seventy-three years, hardly enough to tempt any one to go ambergris hunting.

"And now about the steam-whaling industry. As I mentioned before, the old New England whalers seldom attacked the gray whales, finbacks, and sulphur-bottom whales. This was partly due to the fact that these yielded comparatively little oil, while their whalebone was small and of poor quality. But another reason was that these whales were very difficult to secure by the old-time methods. They are among the largest of whales, are extremely quick in their movements and are powerful swimmers. Moreover, they are shy and wary and always on the alert and are dangerous beyond all other whales when struck.

"Last, but by no means least, they usually sink when killed. But with the invention of harpoon or 'darting' guns, bomb-lances and steam-whaling apparatus the hunting of these whales developed into a large industry which is carried on extensively in Japan, in Scandinavia and on the northwestern coast of the United States. The whales are followed by steamers and are struck with darting- guns and killed with bombs and the bodies are kept from sinking by forcing compressed air into them. After a number are taken, they are towed to shore by the steamers, are skidded or hauled by steam up runways to the factories and practically every portion of them is utilized. Their blubber is boiled for its oil, the livers and other parts also give oil, the hides are used for leather, the bones are ground and the flesh dried and pulverized for fertilizers, or, within recent years, has been butchered and sold in the markets as whale steak. There was a large demand for this meat during the war, especially in the Boston markets, and it really is excellent eating. When we consider that whales are warm-blooded mammals there is no reason why whale meat should not be good, for, contrary to popular ideas, it is neither greasy nor oily and does not taste the least 'fishy.' The whale's oil or fat is all on the outside of the flesh, just as the thick white fat of a hog is between the flesh and the skin, and a whale's meat is not nearly as greasy as that of a hog. In color it is rich, dark red and in flavor it is slightly like veal, or perhaps more like venison.

"Oddly enough, human beings, and especially civilized men, have very strange and absolutely unreasonable prejudices in regard to certain foods, and it is this unaccountable prejudice against eating whales which hitherto has prevented their flesh from being marketed, with the result that countless tons of the most wholesome, tender and well-flavored meat has been thrown away or converted into fertilizer.

"The harpoon-guns, or darting-guns, as whalemen call them, consist of a gun-like arrangement loaded with powder and which fires a harpoon or iron to which a line is attached. There are a great many kinds of these in use and many of the New England whalemen use them at times. Some are designed to be fired from the shoulder, like real guns, while others are swiveled at the bow of the boat on rigid stands or supports. Those used by the steam whalers are usually heavy, cannon-like weapons weighing hundreds of pounds and capable of striking a whale far out of range of the old hand-thrown irons.

"The Yankee whalemen also adopted bomb-lances in the later years of the industry, not only because it decreased the danger to men and boats when killing a whale, but also because it made the death of the whale both quicker and more certain. There were a number of kinds of bomb-lances made and invented, but those commonly in use by the New England whalemen were a combination of harpoon and lance. This weapon consisted of an iron or harpoon of the ordinary pattern attached to a pole while fitted beside it was a gun-like arrangement containing a heavy brass dart tipped with a steel head and fired by a projecting rod which pulled the trigger when driven back. When the iron is thrown at the whale and penetrates his body far enough to be well fast, the rod comes in contact with the creature's skin, thus firing the gun and driving the heavy dart into his vitals. After this is done, the whalemen have only to wait until the whale

THE BOYS' BOOK OF WHALERS

spouts blood, thus avoiding all danger of going in to kill him by the hand-lance. The bomb-lances used by the steam whalers in killing the finbacks are very different. These are guns or cannon which fire an explosive shell or bomb which bursts after it enters the whale's body. Compared with the old New England whalemen's methods such steam whaling must be very unromantic and uninteresting and mere slaughter. It bears just about the same relationship to 'going on' a whale in a frail rowboat, striking him with a hand iron, fighting him until he is tired out and then killing him with a hand-lance, as stalking and killing a grizzly bear with a knife has to sticking pigs in a slaughter-house.

"Nowadays, however, man seeks money rather than romance or adventure, and the steam whaling companies make more profits without risk to life, limb or ships than the old-time whalemen ever dreamed of. Just as the stately old clipper ships gave way to floating palaces of steel and steam; just as the long-bow was laid aside in favor of firearms; just as the stage-coach was superseded by the railway train and the family 'buggy' by the omnipresent Ford, so the staunch old barks, ships and brigs of New England have yielded their place to the steam whaler. The brave-hearted, indomitable, deep-water Yankee skippers have been replaced by captains who could not tell a mainyard from a spanker boom. The roar of a steam whistle is heard where once full-throated sailors sung their chanteys and instead of straining spars and lofty pyramids of sail are throbbing engines and churning screws.

"Before long the last old Yankee whale ship will be but a memory of the past and the last Yankee whalemen will have been laid to rest. We should be thankful that, for a time, the whaling industry of New England has been revived; that once more, for a space, the dingy, smoke-stained sails of the old ships again dot the ocean, that once again crossed yards and wide-spread shrouds rise above New Bedford's water-front and that the war has granted a brief respite to our whale ships and our whalemen."

CHAPTER X

"HOW large were the biggest whales?" asked Harry when the curator ceased speaking. "When you were telling us stories of whalemen's adventures you spoke of an eighty-five foot whale and you mentioned a fifty-foot whale as a mere baby, and in the logs we saw pictures of sixty-barrel and seventy-five-barrel whales."

"It's a hard question to answer," replied the curator. "The whalemen kept records of the number of barrels of oil obtained from the whales they killed, but they seldom bothered to note the length of the creatures. But in some of the logbooks and journals the sizes of whales were recorded, and by comparing the quantity of oil obtained from these with the amounts obtained from others, it is possible to estimate very nearly the size of all whales recorded, and especially of the largest ones. Let me see, here in this logbook, we have two instances of one-hundred-barrel whales being taken. Here is another entry of a whale which yielded one hundred and ten barrels, and we could find scores of others where the whales taken yielded from seventy to ninety barrels each. The largest whale whose measurements I have ever seen entered in a log was a sperm whale which the record says was ninety feet in length, with jaws eighteen feet long and flukes eighteen feet across. Moreover, the quantity of oil taken from this monster is also recorded—one hundred and three barrels. Another log gives the measurements of one whale taken as seventy-nine feet long, jaws sixteen feet long and flukes sixteen feet and six inches across. This whale gave more than the ninety-foot fellow, the yield being one hundred and seven barrels. From these two entries, which are no doubt accurate and reliable, I think you can assume that, to yield one hundred barrels of oil or more, a whale must be about eighty feet in length, and as the proportion of flukes and jaws to the length of the whale is so close in both the instances I have mentioned, we can conclude that the average whale has flukes about as wide as the jaws are long and that a whale's body is about four times as long as its jaws.

THE BOYS' BOOK OF WHALERS

"Many of the whalemen were in the habit of bringing home the jaws of big whales as souvenirs or curios, often using them as archways over the gates to their front gardens, and I know of many jaws still to be found about New Bedford and Nantucket which are sixteen to eighteen feet in length and a short time ago a whale's jaw was offered to the museum which measured twenty-two feet in length. If we can go by the proportions of the whales recorded in the logs, the owner of these jaws must have been at least one hundred and ten feet long—a perfect giant of the seas.

"But this was by no means the biggest of whales known, for in a show-case here we have two sperm whales' teeth which are so enormous that teeth which we know came from an eighty-foot whale appear ridiculously small, and, judging from their size, I should say they came from a whale that certainly must have measured one hundred and fifteen feet in length. I doubt very much if whales ever were taken much larger than this, or at least sperm whales, for I do not know of any records of over one hundred and twenty barrels being taken from any one whale. On the other hand, that is not conclusive proof, for the huge whales were very old,—probably well over one hundred years,—and they were often poor and thin and yielded less oil in proportion to their size than the younger and fatter ones, so that the one-hundred-and-twenty-barrel whale may have been over one hundred and twenty feet long.

"Moreover, we have very little data to guide us in estimating the size of the largest right whales, while the gray whales of the Pacific, which the Yankee whalemen did not hunt, grew to greater size than either the sperm or right whales.

"About all that any one can state with certainty is that in the old whaling days sperm whales seventy-five to one hundred feet long were not uncommon, and unless larger than that they excited no comment.

"To-day, on the other hand, a sixty-foot sperm whale is unusual, and the average yield from sperm whales now taken is about forty barrels each, and while sixty and even seventy barrel whales are occasionally captured, a great many are killed which do not yield over ten or twenty barrels, which indicates whales hardly bigger than a full-grown grampus.

"And, speaking of the size of whales, it is interesting to know that the size and abundance of whales had little if anything to do with the falling off of the old whaling industry. Many people think that the whaling business was largely abandoned because the whales were 'fished out,' so to speak, and that so few whales were left in the oceans that it did not pay to go after them.

"This is a great mistake. Although the whales run smaller than in the old days, owing to the ancient giants having been killed off, yet the whales as a whole are more numerous and are found nearer to our ports than in the times when whale was king in New England. Moreover, the few schooners, barks and brigs that still kept up the industry before the world war took more whales and more oil in short cruises than the old-time ships secured in a cruise of several years. Up to December, 1823, the largest catch of oil taken on a three years' cruise was 2,600 barrels, while in 1830 the *Sarah,* of Nantucket, brought in 3,497 barrels. In 1850 the *Coral* returned from a three years' voyage with 3,500 barrels, while, in 1911, the *Sullivan* obtained 1,500 barrels in *eleven weeks,* and in 1915 the *Cameo* entered New Bedford after a three years' cruise with a cargo of 4,000 barrels, or over 600 barrels more than was ever obtained on a three years' voyage by any of the old whalemen in the zenith of the whaling days.

"Such figures absolutely disprove all statements that whales to-day are scarce or that ships must cruise long distances to find them. The real reason for the decline of the whaling industry was the drop in the prices of whalebone, whale oil, spermaceti and sperm oil, combined with the rise in cost of fitting out, of labor and of ships, while the introduction of steam whaling ships, darting-guns, shore plants, where the blubber was tried out and the offal converted into fertilizers, had practically forced the sailing ships and Yankee whalemen from the seas until the war broke out.

"To illustrate this, let us take the catches I have already mentioned. The 2,600 barrel cargo of 1823 was worth $65,000. The cargo of 3,497 barrels brought in by the *Sarah* was valued at $89,000, and the *Coral's* 3,350 barrels brought

THE REASON FOR THE DECLINE OF THE WHALING INDUSTRY WAS THE DROP IN PRICES OF WHALEBONE AND WHALE OIL

THEY HAD BEEN THROUGH THREE WINTERS IN THE ARCTIC TO SECURE THE FULL CARGO OF OIL

$126,630. But the *Cameo's* 4,000 barrels, on the other hand, were worth only $50,000, or less than one-half the value of the cargo of the *Coral*. From this you can see that if all other things were equal, the modern whaleman, previous to the war, would have to take 10,000 barrels of oil on a three years' cruise in order to make the profits which accrued from a successful voyage in 1850. But even if we assume that it were possible to make such a catch—and it is not— the prices of ships, labor, provisions, supplies and outfit are so much greater to-day than in 1850 that the whaleman's profits from his stupendous catch would be less than he could make at any other calling of the sea.

"For example, the average cost of outfitting a whale ship for a two years' cruise in 1790 was only $12,000. In 1858 it was $65,000, and in 1915 it was $150,000. It was owing to such things that the whaling industry of New England went rapidly to pieces after the discovery and general use of petroleum, the substitution of paraffine and stearine for spermaceti and of artificial bone for whalebone. The whaling business reached its high-water mark in 1850, when New

Bedford and Fairhaven had 314 vessels and nearly 10,000 men devoted to whaling and its fleet each season brought 10,636 barrels of sperm oil, 86,451 barrels of whale oil and 602,100 pounds of whalebone into port. By 1881 the entire whaling fleet of the United States consisted of only 171 vessels, and out of these 123 had New Bedford painted on their counters as their home port.

"And yet the annual catch of this tiny remnant of the old whaling fleet was larger in proportion than ever before. In 1881, 37,614 barrels of sperm oil, 34,626 barrels of whale oil and 458,400 pounds of whalebone were brought in, while in 1915, all that was brought in to New Bedford was 10,000 barrels of sperm oil, while not a pound of bone nor a barrel of right whale oil has entered the port for many years past.

"From 1850 until 1870 the visitor to New Bedford, to Stonington, to New London, or to any one of a score of New England ports could see a forest of masts, a maze of rigging, a labyrinth of spars above the docks where whale ships came and went. Looking across the street here, at Merrill's wharf, you could have seen scores of great barks, ships and brigs, a mountain of oil barrels and an army of men; but by 1915 one would have been obliged to search far and wide to find a square-rigged whale ship in a New England port, and beside old Merrill's wharf a few small Portuguese schooners marked the last of the New Bedford whaling fleet.

"But with the advent of the European war the price of oil once more went up by leaps and bounds. Once again the shipyards, docks and wharves of the old New England whaling ports resounded with the sound of axes, mauls and hammers, of creaking drays and groaning trucks, of squealing winches and of shouts of busy men. From berths on mud flats and at decaying piers, old, half-forgotten hulks were brought forth, overhauled and refitted. Once more came the call for men to go a-whaling, and again, above Merill's wharf and the water-front of many a New England port the heavy masts and long cross yards of stout old whaling ships rose against the sky. Defying wind and weather, laughing at the perils of the sea and of the chase, and scorning lurking submarines, the veteran Yankee whalemen once more stood upon their quarter-decks and sailed their grand old ships upon the seven seas.

"From far and near they sought their cargoes, chasing the sperm whales in the two great oceans, visiting the desolate South Shetlands and Croisettes for sea elephants, pushing their way into frozen seas, and once more the Stars and Stripes flung forth its folds from the mastheads of many a staunch old whale ship.

"But while the price of oil rose to heights never dreamed of in all the years of whaling, still, it was not a profitable business, and comparatively few ships set forth. Food, material, labor and the thousand and one things essential to the whaling business had also reached unheard-of heights in price, and despite the big catches made, the whalemen found it hard to make both ends meet, and in a few years the old ships once more will be abandoned and the little schooners and their Portuguese crews will be the only whalers left to keep alive the memory of New England's old-time fame as the head of the whaling industry.

"In a few more years all the old square-riggers will be again out of commission,—laid up in quiet, out-of-the-way slips or resting immovably upon the mud flats of the ports they served so long and well, for seldom is a whale ship junked,—somehow the owners and the old skippers have a sentimental feeling about their ships and hate to see them destroyed. To them, they are almost like fellow beings,—like the gnarled and knotted old seamen that sailed them,—and they like to feel that the ships which bore them so staunchly and safely around the world and back so many times are resting peacefully in their old age, content to gaze thoughtfully upon the familiar scenes of their home ports and happy in memories of glorious deeds of long ago. And we can scarcely blame the old whalemen for looking upon their ships as almost human. What marvelous stories they could tell if they could speak! What adventures have they not gone through! What storms and seas have they not withstood! For scores of years their keels knew the wide oceans and the far-flung seas. Through the ice-floes of the Arctic and the tepid waters of the tropics their bluff bows have pushed their way. Hard as steel have their dingy sails been frozen by sleet-ladened gales as they rounded Cape Horn and their frayed rigging has oft been coated with gleaming ice in Kamschatkan seas. Far above their lofty mastheads have loomed the pinnacles of stupendous bergs and about their cut-waters have frolicked the rainbow-hued fish of coral-bound lagoons. Under the fir-clad hills of Vancouver they have swung to their anchors and they have moored 'neath the shelter of waving palms. Their grease-soaked decks have felt the patter of naked feet of South Sea cannibals and over their high sides have clambered skin-clad Eskimos. Their scuppers have run red with the blood of men in mortal combat or treacherously slain by mutineers. They have rung to the merry laughter and rollicking songs of the brave whalemen and to the wild yells of savages and the screams of tortured men.

"And what of the men who manned and sailed these ships,—ships such as never again will be built? Like their ships, they, too, are 'out of commission,'—pushed aside by the march of progress and civilization, all but forgotten by the people and the nation which owes them so much.

"In many a song and story we honor our

pioneers of land; we erect handsome monuments and carve lasting memorials to soldier and sailor heroes; but only in one spot—in little New Bedford—will you find a monument to the whalemen. And yet no deeds were ever more worthy of praise than theirs; no braver acts were ever performed by sailor or soldier; no greater aid was ever given to the struggling States than the prosperity brought by the Yankee whalemen.

"They blazed the pathway for civilization and Christianity to the uttermost parts of the earth. They mapped uncharted seas and opened trade routes to commerce. They were the first to look upon many an unknown land, and when their country called to arms they were ever the first to respond. The five oceans and the seven seas were their haunts; in the tropics of the polar regions they were equally at home, but ever their hearts were true to the New England hills and the land whose Stars and Stripes flew at their mastheads.

"But while whaling and the New England whalemen may soon be a thing of the past yet their story, their deeds, their bravery, their skill, even their ships and gear will live on forever and will be seen and wondered at by generations to come. Recently a group of wealthy New England men whose ancestors had been identified with the whaling industry decided to perpetuate the old time whalemen and their ships in such a way that long after the last New England whaleman is dead and the last staunch old whale ship has rotted to pieces and has gone, the public can visualize the life, the chase, the dangers, the courage and the adventures of the old-time whalemen. A few books had been written on the subject, many paintings and photographs had been made, but books do not last forever and never reach more than a small portion of the world, so in order to make the story of the whaler more widely known and to make the life of the whalemen more realistic, it was decided to have a motion picture made of a whaling voyage. Not just a few short scenes of various events, but a consecutive, thrilling story, a story filled with romance, adventure and suspense; a story with a well-defined plot which would interest anyone and yet a story which would portray every detail of a whaling voyage from the time the ship was fitted out until it again sailed into port weather-beaten, buffeted, but with a full cargo of oil.

"To be sure that the tale might be absolutely accurate, all the old records of New Bedford, Nantucket and other famous old whaling ports were searched, the logs and journals and the collections in the museum here were studied, old whalemen were consulted and the story written. Then came the question of ships. No modern schooner, no up-to-date steam whaler, no bomb lances or darting guns would serve. The story and the film must depict only the real old-time ship and the old hand methods. Luckily the ships were available and fortunately, too, there were still enough old-time whalemen left to man ships and boats and go a-whaling as in the good old days. As a most fitting beginning the opening scenes were taken on the oldest whaling vessel in existence—the bark *Chas. W. Morgan*, built in 1841. For years the old hulk had lain upon the mud flats across the harbor at Fairhaven, deserted, abandoned and almost forgotten with grass and weeds growing from her seams and upon her decks. Then, in 1915, with the rise of oil due to the war the staunch old ship was dragged from her long resting place, she was caulked, repaired, refitted, and fully manned sailed forth from New Bedford as though risen from the grave. No one who saw her would have ever guessed that the trim, freshly painted ship with her long yards, her taut rigging, her great white sails and her fluttering flags which rode so majestically at anchor in the bay was the same dilapidated old wreck which had been a landmark of Fairhaven's water-front for years. But as I have already told you, whale ships in the old days were built to last forever and outward from New Bedford's harbor the rejuvenated *Morgan* sailed to breast the long swells of the Atlantic, to swelter under the equatorial sun of the doldrums, to battle under reefed topsails with the storm-lashed Antarctic, for the *Morgan's* destination was the South Shetland Islands where she was to hunt sea elephants. And as bravely as ever the old ship held her own. Through storm and calm she bore steadily southward; she reached the bleak and God-forsaken isles close to the South Pole and safely back she came to her home port with her catch of oil and a goodly quantity of ambergris besides.

THE BOYS' BOOK OF WHALERS

"So, upon the *Morgan's* decks the first pictures were taken and then another ship,—indistinguishable and second only to the *Morgan* in point of age and fame—the *Gaspé*—was fitted for the cruise. Manned by old-time whalemen, equipped to the last detail exactly as she had been years ago, the *Gaspé* sailed for the sperm-whale grounds of the tropical Atlantic, while upon her were the motion-picture men with their cameras. Somewhere in the Caribbean or on the Atlantic between Africa and the West Indies the *Gaspé* is cruising for 'sparm,' her boats are being lowered, her men are pulling the long ash oars in pursuit of the monsters of the sea, her boat-steerers are heaving the heavy irons as their ancestors did generations ago; her mates are risking life and limb and instant death is standing ever at their elbows as they creep in and shove home the lance. Again the cry of 'fin up' is ringing over the Atlantic; again the black sooty smoke from the try-works is rising from the deck of a New Bedford whale ship beneath the blue tropic sky. Once more the great blanket-pieces are being stripped from the whale, the huge jaw is being hoisted aboard and the spermaceti is being baled from the case. And between whiles, as of old, the men are skylarking on deck, they are scrimshawing teeth, carving curios from bone, dancing in the moonlight to the music of a mouth organ and a battered accordion. All is being recorded, all is being pictured and made permanent. Nothing is missing save the brutality and the abuses, the cruelty and the oaths and, perhaps, to make the scenes even more realistic, a bit of these will be staged as well."

www.ingramcontent.com/pod-product-compliance
Lightning Source LLC
LaVergne TN
LVHW041614070426
835507LV00008B/237